Lectionary Scenes

57 Vignettes
For
Cycle A

Robert F. Crowley

CSS Publishing Company, Inc., Lima, Ohio

LECTIONARY SCENES, CYCLE A

Library of Congress Cataloging-in-Publication Data

Crowley, Robert F., 1938-
    Lectionary scenes : 56 vignettes for Cycle C / Robert F. Crowley.
       p.   cm.
    ISBN 0-7880-1060-3 (paperback)
    1. Drama in Christian education. 2. Drama in public worship. 3. Bible plays. 4. Christian drama, American. 5. Common lectionary (1992)   I. Title.
BV289.C76   1997
246'.72—DC21   96-46497
                                                         CIP

This book is available in the following formats, listed by ISBN:
      0-7880-1273-8   Book
      0-7880-1274-6   IBM
      0-7880-1275-4   MAC
      0-7880-1276-2   Sermon Prep

PRINTED IN U.S.A.

To the only God of Creativity, the Father, Son, and Holy Spirit.

To Suanne, my wonderful, understanding, helpful wife and friend.

To Lion Players and Fisherpeople Drama Ministry, who breathed life into these vignettes.

Table Of Contents

Preface   11

Introduction   13

First Sunday In Advent   15
Matthew 24:37-44
Like A Thief

Second Sunday In Advent   22
Matthew 3:1-12
Bible Trivia

Third Sunday In Advent   30
Matthew 11:2-11
Holy Hype

Fourth Sunday In Advent   34
Matthew 1:18-25
Mr. Roberts And The Christmas Tree

Christmas Day   39
Luke 2:1-14
Orders Are Orders

Epiphany   45
Matthew 2:1-12
The Last Wise Man

First Sunday After Epiphany   48
Matthew 3:13-17
When

Second Sunday After Epiphany 53
John 1:29-41
Job Placement

Third Sunday After Epiphany 60
Matthew 4:12-23
To Climb A Mountain

Fourth Sunday After Epiphany 64
Matthew 5:1-12
Be About It

Fifth Sunday After Epiphany 73
Matthew 5:13-20
You And The Law

Sixth Sunday After Epiphany 78
Matthew 5:21-24, 27-30, 33-37
Robin Hood?

Seventh Sunday After Epiphany 85
Matthew 5:38-48
The Tooth Fairy

Eighth Sunday After Epiphany 92
Matthew 6:24-34
Servant And Two Masters

Transfiguration Of Our Lord 96
Matthew 17:1-9
A Light Verse

First Sunday In Lent 102
Matthew 4:1-11
Fasting

Second Sunday In Lent 106
John 3:1-17
The Night Talker

Third Sunday In Lent   111
    John 4:5-42
    A Drink Of Water

Fourth Sunday In Lent   115
    John 9:1-38
    A Blind Man Sees

Fifth Sunday In Lent   121
    John 11:1-44
    Talk Show II

Second Sunday Of Easter   125
    John 20:19-31
    Life

Third Sunday Of Easter   130
    Luke 24:13-35
    Walk With Him

Fourth Sunday Of Easter   134
    Acts 6:1-9
    The Church

Fifth Sunday Of Easter   145
    John 14:1-14
    In My Father's House

Sixth Sunday Of Easter   148
    Psalm 148
    Creation

Seventh Sunday Of Easter   153
    John 17:1-11
    Everyman And Woman

Day Of Pentecost   160
    Acts 2:1-11
    The Lord, The Holy Spirit

Holy Trinity   **169**
Matthew 28:16-20
The Lesser Commission

Proper 1   **174**
Matthew 5:21-24, 27-30, 33-37
AIDS

Proper 2   **180**
Matthew 5:38-48
The Inmate

Proper 3   **185**
Matthew 6:24-34
Fatherhood

Proper 4   **188**
Matthew 7:21-27
House On Sand

Proper 5   **191**
Matthew 9:9-13
Super Christian I

Proper 6   **195**
Matthew 9:35—10:8 (9-15)
The Elevator

Proper 7   **202**
Matthew 10:24-33
The Bible Study

Proper 8   **212**
Matthew 10:34-42
O.J.T.

Proper 9   **218**
Matthew 11:25-30
The Future Of The Church!

Proper 10   226
    Matthew 13:1-9, 18-23
    The Sower And The Seed And So What

Proper 11   230
    Matthew 13:24-30, 36-43
    Showdown

Proper 12   236
    Matthew 13:31-33, 44-49
    Before The Wedding

Proper 13   240
    Matthew 14:13-21
    Feeding The 4999

Proper 14   246
    Matthew 14:22-33
    Water Logged

Proper 15   253
    Matthew 15:21-28
    Demonized

Proper 16   258
    Matthew 16:13-20
    Who Is God?

Proper 17   266
    Matthew 16:21-27
    The One Chosen

Proper 18   271
    Matthew 18:15-20
    My Brother's Keeper

Proper 19   274
    Matthew 18:21-35
    The King Forgives Sometimes

Proper 20   278
    Matthew 20:1-16
    Pay Day

Proper 21   283
    Matthew 21:28-32
    Knock, Knock!

Proper 22   288
    Matthew 21:33-43
    The Wicked Pie Bakers

Proper 23   293
    Matthew 22:1-14
    Many Are Called

Proper 24   298
    Matthew 22:15-22
    God And The State

Proper 25   302
    Matthew 22:34-46
    David The Giant Killer

Proper 26   312
    Matthew 23:1-12
    In His Debt

Proper 27   319
    Matthew 25:1-13
    No Honeymoon

Proper 28   327
    Matthew 25:14, 15, 19-29
    The Parable Of Big Business

Proper 29   334
    Matthew 25:31-46
    The Glory Of The Lord

Preface

For me, the greatest test of a dramatic work is whether the audience reacts to it as the playwright intended. These scenes have passed that test, some of them many times. Members of the audiences who have enjoyed them have requested their favorites over the years. My hope is that when you do them they will be often requested. They are to be enjoyed by actors, directors, and audiences and, I hope, by God.

Introduction

You probably want to act or direct or somehow help produce one or more of these scenes for your church or church-related group. Great! It is possible.

Every human being has the inherent ability to act. God, in His wisdom, created us in His image and therefore we are creative. As actors, directors, or producers of drama, God allows us to co-create with Him. This is a privilege and a responsibility.

Prayer

Talking to God comes first. Do it a lot! Every time there's a snag — pray. Pray as much as you rehearse.

Rehearsal

A lot of rehearsal is necessary for a good performance. A ratio of 40-to-1 is not unreasonable. That means for every minute you are performing you need forty minutes of rehearsal. This does not count memorizing your lines before rehearsal.

Humility

Don't become proud! It is easy for creative people to fall into this trap. Don't let it happen to you. Remember, God used Balaam's donkey to speak for Him. God can use anyone in a drama ministry who is willing to learn and who is obedient.

Awareness

Be alert to the wiles of the Devil. He will attack you before, during, or after the ministry. Pray! Protect yourself. Pray for each other.

Competitiveness

You are not in competition with other members of your troupe. You are their brother or sister in Christ. Treat them as honored members of Jesus' body.

Ministry

Acting these scenes is a ministry, not a performance. The Lord God allows us to minister for Him to others and He also allows us to minister to Him. It is a sacred duty.

God is always teaching me His ways. He will teach you, too. I'm thankful He wants to use all of us. God bless your efforts.

Like A Thief

Theme

We can be so heavenly minded that we are no earthly good.

Summary

Minny, a Christian woman, is preparing for bed as a thief enters. She mistakes the thief for Jesus coming back to take her to heaven. Dan, the thief, takes the opportunity to rob her of everything of value in the house.

Playing Time	4-5 minutes
Setting	A neutral playing area that represents Minny's home, with a screen for the thief to hide behind
Props	A black garbage bag
Costumes	Minny — Pajamas, bathrobe, hair curlers
	Dan — all black clothes and black sneakers
Time	The present
Cast	MINNY — a Christian woman
	DAN — a thief

MINNY: (*ENTERS DRESSED FOR BED, HAIR UP IN CURLERS*) Why can't he ever check the doors? What is it with this guy? He gets to bed and all he can think about is sleep.

I remember how he used to talk to me for hours on the phone when we were dating — now if I get so much as a "I'm home," from him I'm lucky. Yesterday all he said to me was, "While you're up, will you get me a glass of root beer and change the channel?"

He's a psychiatrist, for Pete's sake. He talks to people all day. He solves their problems. That's it. That's the answer. I should visit him at his office and pay him. Maybe he'd talk to me then.

Let's see, I checked the back door. Is the cat in? She's probably down in the basement.

Doggone you, Bill, you sleepy head. I wanted to tell you about what Bob Devine said on the radio today, about the end times, about how the Lord was going to come back. And what do I do? I end up talking to myself.

Bob Devine said no one knows when Jesus might return. It could be any time. And we must be prepared for His return, he said. He didn't say how we should prepare, though.

Did I check the front door? I better look for the cat out front and then I'll lock the basement door. (*SHE EXITS*)

DAN: (*ENTERS. HE IS A BURGLAR, CARRYING A BAG FOR HIS LOOT*) Good thing that basement door was open. Some people make it so easy for me. This looks like a likely place. Lots of silver. Probably lots of jewelry too. Oh oh, I guess they're still up roaming around. I better make myself scarce. I hope they dust. I'm allergic to dust. (*HE DUCKS BEHIND A SCREEN AS MINNY ENTERS BUT IN HIS HASTE DROPS HIS BAG.*)

MINNY: That cat must be in here somewhere. Here, kitty, kitty. Oh well, let her stay out all night, we can probably give the kittens away to someone. (*FINDING DAN'S BAG*) What's this doing here? Doggone you, Bill, there can't be a sloppier husband than you. Just an empty bag. (*DAN SNEEZES*)

Lord? Is that you? Did you come for me, Lord? This is it, huh, Lord? What do you want me to do? Do you want me to wake Bill up?

DAN: Uh, no, no, don't do that!

MINNY: But don't you want to take him to heaven, too?

DAN: Who, me? Uh, gee, I don't know.

16

MINNY: Do you mean you're just taking me?

DAN: Uh, yeah, I guess so.

MINNY: Lord, you're a little unsure of yourself. Lord, what's bothering you? Is it because I haven't read my Bible like I said I was going to? Is that it? I usually remember to pray every day. I've got Bill used to prayer before meals. That's pretty good, isn't it, Lord? (*NO ANSWER*) Lord? Are you still there?

DAN: Yeah, sure. I was just thinking.

MINNY: Oh, that's all right, Lord. You were probably thinking about whether I should wake Bill or not, right. He'll be awful mad if he wakes up in the morning and I haven't cooked his oatmeal for him. He loves his hot oatmeal in the morning, with a little milk in it and butter ...

DAN: No, no, that's all right. We don't want to bother him.

MINNY: Oh, I get it. You want people to be watching for your coming all the time so they'll be ready, like I was ready for you tonight. That sleepy head Bill was not ready was he? Well, I'm ready to go. (*CLOSING HER EYES AND EXPECTING SOMETHING TO HAPPEN. NOTHING DOES*) Lord, I'm ready to do whatever you tell me to do. What do you want me to do?

DAN: Uh, I don't know. Uh, well, let's see. You might start by filling up that bag, there ...

MINNY: This one?

DAN: Yes, that's it. Just fill that up with your best silver and jewelry.

MINNY: Are you kidding? Oh, sorry, Lord. Of course you're not kidding. I didn't mean that. My silver? My jewelry? Why?

17

DAN: Uh, gee, uh, need you ask?

MINNY: Oh, I get it. You're testing me. Just like you tested Abraham. I know. You're going to provide a ram in the bushes, aren't you?

DAN: Huh?

MINNY: The ram in the bushes. You know.

DAN: Oh, the getaway car. Yeah, it's running outside.

MINNY: Oh, Lord, you're so clever. I didn't dream you'd be so, well, uh, down to earth, so natural. I thought you'd speak in "thees" and "thous" and say things like "verily, verily, I say unto thee." But you're so, uh, like one of us. Well, you would be, wouldn't you? You are one of us, so to speak. Getaway car, that's good. That's how we're going home, eh? How cute, a getaway car. Oh, I better get busy with my jewelry and silver. Anything else I should put in the bag?

DAN: Well, do you have any coins?

MINNY: Yes, you know we do. Bill has that old coin collection in the safe. He never gets it out any more. You know how he loves that collection. He says it's worth millions. Why of course you'd want that, wouldn't you. You want us to love you more than silver or gold. I get it. I get it.

DAN: Well, get it!

MINNY: Oh, Lord, you're so funny. Okay, okay. Oh, it's going to be such fun in heaven with you. You'll be cracking jokes all eternity. All the saints will be rolling in the clouds. I bet you keep the angels in stitches. (*SHE EXITS*)

DAN: (*APPEARING FROM BEHIND SCREEN*) Boy, oh boy. What a dame. She's driving me crazy. But it's the first time I get the help of the victim. Maybe I ought to just rob Christians from now on. I liked the bit about the ram in the bushes. (*LAUGHING TO HIMSELF*) Getaway car. (*LAUGHING*) Oh, here she is back again. (*HE DUCKS BEHIND THE SCREEN*)

MINNY: (*ENTERS*) Hey, Lord. I was talking to you. Why can't you hear me when I'm in the other room? Oh, I get it. It must be because when we had those Bible studies we had them in here. Well, anyway. I wondered if you wanted all our credit cards?

DAN: Uh, yeah. Why not?

MINNY: That's what I thought you'd say. Why not! (*EMPTY-ING HER WALLET OF CREDIT CARDS*) Oh, I almost forgot, here's some loose bills I had and I cleaned out Bill's wallet too. I even know where he keeps some money hidden away in the freezer. Of course you knew that, didn't you? Well, here it all is in the bag. I guess I'm about ready to go. I decided not to take the time to fix my hair or change clothes or anything. I guess you know me pretty well, huh, Lord? Well, like I say, I'm ready. (*SHE CLOSES HER EYES EXPECTING SOMETHING TO HAPPEN. DAN STEALS OUT FROM BEHIND THE SCREEN AND TRIES TO TAKE THE BAG BUT MINNY IS HOLDING IT TIGHTLY. HE RETURNS TO HIS HIDING PLACE*)

DAN: Uh, you'll have to let the bag go, now.

MINNY: Let it go?

DAN: Yes, let it go.

MINNY: Oh, I get it. We have to release all our worldly posses-sions into your loving hands.

DAN: Yeah, you might say that.

MINNY: Okay, I'm releasing it all to you, Lord.

DAN: Good. Now, just relax and remember to keep your eyes closed.

MINNY: Okay. Oh, I get it. You want me to soar through the clouds but you're afraid I might get sick. Sure, Lord. I'm ready. (*DAN BEGINS TO EXIT*) Ohhh, it does feel like I'm flying. Yes, of course I am.

DAN: Don't open your eyes. Don't look down. Keep your eyes shut. There, that's a good little Christian. Keep your eyes shut. Good. Good.

MINNY: Lord, it seems like your voice is getting farther away. Why is that?

DAN: (*RUNNING BACK BEHIND THE SCREEN*) Because .... uh ....

MINNY: Oh, I get it. I have to trust that you are there even when I can't hear you.

DAN: Yes, that's it exactly. Now, just trust me and keep your eyes closed.

MINNY: Oh, I will. But, Lord, won't you say something to me, something I can remember in heaven?

DAN: Huh? Oh sure. Uh, how about this, "The Lord helps those who help themselves."

MINNY: Oh, that's wonderful. I'll remember that. You helped yourself, didn't you? Yes, I'll remember. (*DAN EXITS*)
  Oh, such a feeling. A feeling of lightness. Unfettered by worldly things. Oh, it's wonderful.

20

So this is heaven. (*SHE OPENS HER EYES*) Oh, how lovely. It is truly beautiful. The air is so fresh and clean. Isn't that just like the Lord to make heaven just like my house so I wouldn't have the ultimate cultural shock.

And I just bet the Lord brought Bill along, too. I'll just tiptoe upstairs to wake that sleepy head. Won't he be surprised when he finds out he's in heaven? *(AS SHE EXITS)*

The Lord helps those who help themselves. Hmm.

Bible Trivia

Theme

What are some of the interesting facts about the life of John the Baptist?

Summary

Four friends are playing "Bible Trivia" and learn something about John the Baptist.

Playing Time	5 minutes
Setting	A neutral playing area that represents a living room
Props	A "Bible Trivia" game
Costumes	Contemporary
Time	The present
Cast	JIM — and his friends:
	MARY
	JOHN
	SANDY

(*THE PLAYERS ARE RETURNING TO BIBLE TRIVIA AFTER A BREAK*)

JIM: It's your turn.

MARY: I hate this game.

JOHN: You only hate it because you never win.

MARY: Well, that's true enough. I can't even answer one question, it seems.

SANDY: Can we just play, please.

JIM: Yes, let's get back to it.

MARY: Oh, all right. Whose turn is it?

SANDY: It's yours.

MARY: Oh. (*PICKING A CARD*)

JIM: (*LOOKING AT CARD*) Oh, man, this is so easy. Why don't I ever get the easy ones?

MARY: Who was it that said, "I am not even fit to stoop down and untie the thong of His sandals"?

JOHN: A shoe salesman with a poor self image.

MARY: Do you want me to read the question again?

SANDY: Yes, please.

JOHN: No, we got the question. What we want is the answer.

MARY: Are you giving up?

JOHN: No, we're not giving up!

SANDY: I'm no good with quotations.

MARY: Who was it that said, "I am not even fit to stoop down and untie the thong of His sandals"?

SANDY: Tell us who it was he was talking about.

MARY: I can't do that. We agreed there would be no hints.

SANDY: Jim got a hint on that Narcissus question.

MARY: He couldn't answer it anyway.

JIM: That one was a mistake. I heard that there were mistakes in this game. Time's up anyway.

JOHN: No. It can't be.

JIM: Who's the time keeper?

JOHN: You are but you're a lousy one.

SANDY: I give up.

MARY: Do you give up, John?

JOHN: No. Not yet.

JIM: I said time's up.

JOHN: And I heard you.

JIM: Well, what does that mean to you?

JOHN: It means — get out of my face. I'm thinking, all right!

JIM: Just admit you don't know.

JOHN: Okay, what's the answer?

JIM AND MARY: John the Baptist!

MARY: Let's quit this stupid game. We could watch a movie.

JIM: No. We're playing.

MARY: I never know any of the answers.

JIM: That's what we're doing. We're learning.

MARY: I'm not learning. I'm getting frustrated and bored. Who was John the Baptist, anyway?

JOHN: He founded the Baptist Church.

JIM: John the Baptist was the guy who lived in the wilderness and preached about the coming of the Messiah.

SANDY: The Messiah? Oh, Jesus!

JIM: Right, Jesus, but no one knew Jesus was the Messiah until He was baptized by his cousin, John.

MARY: John the Baptist was the cousin of Jesus?

JIM: Right.

JOHN: And he wore a fur coat, didn't he?

SANDY: A fur coat? Are you kidding?

JIM: Kinda like a fur coat. He wore a covering of camel's skin.

SANDY: It doesn't sound so glamorous now.

JOHN: John the Baptist ate grasshoppers and honey. Probably in a very gooey, crunchy sandwich.

MARY: Let's watch the movie. This is getting ridiculous.

JOHN: Well, he really did.

SANDY: He did not, did he, Jim? You're the expert.

JIM: Well, not quite. The Bible mentions that he ate locusts and wild honey but the locusts were probably the beans from the carob bush or honey locust tree.

MARY: How do you know all this stuff?

JIM: I was there.

JOHN: Oh, right.

JIM: No, really. I go to a Bible study.

SANDY: But how can you remember all this detail?

JOHN: He didn't know the "Narcissus" answer.

JIM: I told you that was a mistake.

JOHN: Sure it was.

MARY: All right. Who cares. I just want to watch a movie.

JOHN: I bet you don't know what John the Baptist and Smokey the Bear had in common.

SANDY: I bet this is going to be profound.

JIM: No, what?

JOHN: They both had the same middle name!

MARY: I know what movie I'm going to watch.

JOHN: Don't tell us. *The Sound of Music*, right?

MARY: I'm not going to tell you.

SANDY: You can't quit. Jim needs a partner.

JIM: That's all right. I'll take you two on alone.

JOHN: This ought to be good.

JIM: And I'll probably win, too.

JOHN: Yeah. Right.

SANDY: Just so we don't have to listen to any more stories about eating grasshoppers.

JIM: He didn't eat grasshoppers.

JOHN: Prove it.

JIM: Let's get on with the game.

JOHN: You can't prove it, can you?

JIM: No, I can't.

JOHN: You see!

SANDY: You see!

MARY: You see!

JIM: "Oh, you brood of vipers!"

JOHN: Whoa! What is this?

JIM: It's just something John the Baptist said and it seemed to fit this situation.

MARY: Oh, no.

SANDY: Can we get back to the game.

JOHN: You've got a lot of nerve calling me a viper.

JIM: You, especially, are a viper.

JOHN: I was a "vindow viper" this week.

SANDY: Cute.

JIM: Let's get back to the game.

SANDY: Yeah.

MARY: So, why was John the Baptist important?

JOHN: I thought you were going to watch a movie.

MARY: I couldn't find one I liked.

JIM: John the Baptist's mission was to prepare the way for Jesus.

MARY: Why would Jesus, who was the Son of God, need any way prepared for Him?

JIM: Well, I don't know, but He did.

JOHN: I thought you were going to tell us something important.

JIM: His message was to make way for Jesus. He told the people to repent.

MARY: Repent?

JIM: Repent in Hebrew means to change your heart.

MARY: I guess it's still a message the world could use today. "Change your heart — Jesus is coming."

JIM: You're right.

JOHN: To change your heart in preparation for whatever Jesus wants to do in your heart. I get it.

MARY: Sounds like something everyone could use in the game of life.

SANDY: Let's watch a movie. (*JOHN, MARY AND SANDY EXIT*)

JIM: Hey, wait. What about the game? Okay, I win. You forfeit the game. I win!

Holy Hype

Theme

We can miss the man, Jesus, if we become enthralled with His works. We can miss the Father if we cannot see Jesus.

Summary

A slick public relations person is telephoning Jesus to set up a glitzy itinerary to promote Jesus' ministry. Jesus tells him He doesn't need that. (A monologue)

Playing Time	3 minutes
Setting	Anywhere
Props	A mobile phone
Costumes	A sharp suit
Time	The present
Cast	HARRY (Actually, this character could be male or female)

HARRY: (*ON THE PHONE*) Hello, uh, hello. This is Mr. Hastings, Harry Hastings from Hastings Promotions. Put me through to Jesus. He's what? What! Praying? Oh, no, that just won't do. Huh? Oh, nothing.

Well, of course He knows me. Yes, we did do lunch together last week. Don't worry. He'll remember me. Hastings Promotions, yes. Please, if I could just talk to Him for a minute. I have some things I want Him to approve. Yes, yes, I'll wait. (*PAUSE. HARRY TALKS TO HIMSELF*)

Boy, I don't know. These guys get on top and they forget who put them there. (*JESUS COMES TO THE PHONE*)

Oh, hello, Jesus, baby, listen. I got some great ideas. I think you're slipping just bit in the ratings so give a listen. I think we ought to do a television special. Sure, a special, an hour long. Here's the way I see it shaping up. It will be called "My Jerusalem." You know, one of those tour-of-the-city things featuring you. It'll be great for your ministry. We'll have some shots of the Gates and then you can recall your Triumphal Entry. We can fill in with some footage of that. We'll do something from the temple. No, no, not inside the Temple. Just an outside shot. We don't want to mention anything about the fracas you started in there. I think we can just gloss over that. You'll say some nice things about how your ministry is not in opposition to that of the Temple — you are more of an evangelist.

Anyway you get the picture. We'll have some music of course and some of that ethnic dancing, you know, from a wedding and then you could mention your first miracle, you know the water into wine bit. All the details haven't been worked out as yet but it looks pretty good. I personally think this is going to do something for your campaign. *(PAUSE)*

Oh yeah? Well, never mind. But listen, Jesus, listen to this. I personally am going to handle this. Huh? No, no more mess ups. Sure, sure. I admit the article about John the Baptist was a bit strong, but we had to play up the unique attire, if you know what I mean. Don't worry. I talked to Johnson about that article. I myself didn't write that, but well, yes, Sir — of course, John is in Herod's jail but you must admit he was a little too outspoken. I told him just to read the statement I prepared but he wouldn't do it.

But that's not why I called. Now, listen, Jesus, you've got to change your image. The way you're handling things is not working. People aren't believing it. It's too radical, too strong. You really can't go into the signs and wonders bit, that's too much. People just don't go for that anymore. Trust me in this. I know you can talk about the wine miracle and feeding the five thousand but you have got to stop doing the healing stuff. Healing the blind, and the lame and cleansing lepers, and the deaf hearing. It's a bit too much. If the people are there live they believe, but it just doesn't carry on T.V. People know we can edit the tape. And raising the dead — forget that one altogether. No one, but no one, will ever believe that even if they are there.

I tell you what we could do. Sure, we could have you turn some water into wine and feed a bunch of people with five loaves and a couple of fish. People will go for that. I'm working with a manufacturer right now on a new line of toys with pitchers that turn water into wine, well, it's not really wine. We don't want to make winos out of children.

Anyway, listen. It should be a big seller. And maybe we can have a line of Jesus wines. We'll have to work on that. Here's the new bit. You come out in a suit with a decent haircut and of course you'll want to do something about that beard. No, now, listen to me. I know what the public is buying. Beards are out. They really are. Clean shaven — that's the ticket. We've got to appeal to the young people. That's the trend. Okay, just trust me on this.

Now, Jesus, baby, listen. All right — you're in the spotlight — the cameras are rolling and I have this wacked out speech that will have them in your pocket. It's great, you'll see. Now, listen, this speech, yeah, I wrote it myself. I think it combines just the right amount of humor to warm up the audience and then we have some salient points and examples and I wrote some of those parables that you like to tell. And then you end up with a teary-eyed appeal for a conclusion that will melt even the hardest heart and get those people to part with some of that green stuff. After all that's what it's all about, isn't it? We have to keep the money pouring in so the ministry will continue.

Huh? Well, of course it's not your style, but that's what we're changing. We're working on your image, here. No more back-woods preacher. No sir. You're going to be a snappy dressing Madison Avenue type.

Hold on, now, let me finish. As I said you come out and make your speech, promise a few things like food for the poor and then we have the appeal. That's what gets them — the appeal. I tell you you'll have them in your pocket.

Well, listen, I have to go. But I'll get back to you and have you sign some papers. What? Why, of course, we'll do lunch next week when I'm in town. What do you mean, don't bother? Oh, don't bother to bring the papers, but Jesus, I don't think I can sell you without changing the image.

You want to keep the old one? Why? Because you're the exact image of the Father? I don't get it.

Mr. Roberts And
The Christmas Tree

Theme

Christmas is a time to celebrate Jesus. And what better way than to decorate a Christmas tree with decorations that are a witness to Jesus and our relationship with Him.

Summary

Mr. Roberts orders a Christmas tree and some decorations but he isn't prepared for a talking Christmas tree. The tree explains to Mr. Roberts the importance of Jesus and our relationship to God.

Playing Time	4 minutes
Setting	The television studio of Mr. Roberts
Props	Fish bowl and fish
	Picture (with "Xmas" written on it)
	Box with Christmas tree inside
	Christmas tree decorations (garland, ornaments, angel, star)
	Christmas cookies on a plate
Costumes	Mr. Roberts — suit coat and tie, sweater, cardigan, street shoes, tennis shoes
	Mr. McDoley — delivery uniform with cap, delivery bag
Cast	MR. ROBERTS
	MR. McDOLEY
	TREE

Production Notes: We used a special tree that was sound activated and placed it in front of an amplifier. When the "tree" spoke it also moved. This might not always be possible.

MR. ROBERTS: *(MUSIC UP AS MR. ROBERTS ENTERS AND CHANGES INTO HIS TV COSTUME)* Oh, come on in. Sit down. We can have a little talk with each other.

Since the last time we met I thought about you a lot. Uh-huh. I did. I was cooking something for myself the other evening and I thought, my goodness, I'd like to share this with my friend. Uh-huh. And now you're here and we can share something together. Would you like that? Well, so would I. Let's check out what the picture says. Well, what's this? It says "XMAS." Do you all see that? "XMAS." X-M-A-S. What does it mean? It means Christmas, doesn't it. That's right. We'll talk more about Christmas later. *(DOOR BELL RINGS)*

Oh, oh, someone's coming to call. Who do you think it is? I was expecting Mr. McDoley but it is a bit early for his delivery. What do you think? I better go see who it is. *(LOOKING OUT WINDOW)* It is. It is Mr. McDoley. I better let him in.

MR. McDOLEY: Good day. Good day, Mr. Roberts. Good day. A busy day today. It's Christmas Eve, today, you know, Mr. Roberts.

MR. ROBERTS: Yes, I know. We were just going to talk about Christmas, Mr. McDoley

MR. McDOLEY: You were? Oh, that's nice, Mr. Roberts. That's really nice.

MR. ROBERTS: Would you like to stay and talk with us about Christmas, Mr. McDoley?

MR. McDOLEY: Why, I'd love to, Mr. Roberts, but I've got more deliveries than ever today. I mustn't be late, you know. Goodbye, and Merry Christmas to you.

MR. ROBERTS: Mr. McDoley, aren't you forgetting your delivery?

MR. MCDOLEY: Oh, my goodness. I almost forgot, didn't I? I do have a delivery for you, Mr. Roberts.

35

MR. ROBERTS: Is it what I ordered?

MR. McDOLEY: I think it is, Mr. Roberts. I think it is. I have it right here. (*HE PRODUCES A BOX*)

MR. ROBERTS: Good. This is right on time, Mr. McDoley. I was just going to talk about Christmas.

MR. McDOLEY: Here you are, Mr. Roberts. I have one Christmas tree.

MR. ROBERTS: That's right. That's what I ordered, one Christmas tree.

MR. McDOLEY: All righty. I've got to go.

MR. ROBERTS: Mr. McDoley. How much is this delivery?

MR. McDOLEY: That's just "one," today, Mr. Roberts. All righty?

MR. ROBERTS: All right, here you are, Mr. McDoley. Here is "one."

MR. McDOLEY: "One." Thank you, Mr. Roberts. I'll be running along, now. A very special busy day, today.

MR. ROBERTS: Wait, a minute, Mr. McDoley. I wanted you to have a Christmas cookie that I baked just the other evening.

MR. McDOLEY: All righty, Mr. Roberts. I will take just one. And Merry Christmas to you Mr. Roberts. (*EXITS*)

MR. ROBERTS: And a Merry Christmas to you, too, Mr. McDoley. Isn't Mr. McDoley a nice man. He's busy, of course, but he always takes time to say, "Hi." I like that.

   Wasn't Mr. McDoley nice to give me some decorations for my Christmas tree? Now, let's decorate the tree. Would you like that? I've been looking forward to it all week long. Now, what's the first thing I should put on the tree? I know. I'll hang this garland.

CHRISTMAS TREE: Thank you.

MR. ROBERTS: Well, my, my, this is interesting. A talking Christmas tree. I wasn't expecting that, were you?

CHRISTMAS TREE: That strand you just put on me felt good. It dressed me up so I can show forth light for Christmas.

MR. ROBERTS: Show forth light?

CHRISTMAS TREE: Sure. It's what I'm supposed to do. I shine for Jesus at Christmas time.

MR. ROBERTS: I didn't know that. Did you know that?

CHRISTMAS TREE: Well, it's true. Who created trees?

MR. ROBERTS: Well, God did.

CHRISTMAS TREE: Of course. God created trees and you, Mr. Roberts, and everyone. And we can choose to shine for Him.

MR. ROBERTS: That's right, we can choose to shine for Jesus. I want to shine for Jesus, don't you? What shall I put on next? I know, I'll add some of these ornaments. See how shiny they are?

CHRISTMAS TREE: They are lights in a dark world. Every time we do something that is good or tell the truth or obey our parents it is a light in a dark world.

MR. ROBERTS: Oh, I want to be a light shining in a dark world. I'll bet you do too. And look what we have now. An angel. I know what this is for. For the angels that sang "Hallelujah" when Jesus was born.

CHRISTMAS TREE: Right you are, Mr. Roberts. The Bible says there was a whole army of angels telling the world that Jesus was born.

MR. ROBERTS: I would liked to have seen that. Would you like to see angels and hear them singing?

CHRISTMAS TREE: Do you know what, Mr. Roberts? We all can be just like those angels and tell everyone about Jesus being born.

MR. ROBERTS: Yes, yes, we can all do that. Let's not forget the star. It goes on top.

CHRISTMAS TREE: The star of Bethlehem, pointing the way to Jesus.

MR. ROBERTS: Now, look. I'm going to point to Jesus, just like the star of Bethlehem did. (*HE POINTS TO HIS HEART*) You see? Let's all point to our heart. Jesus is in our heart if we ask Him to live there. Jesus in our heart. Uh-huh. Isn't that wonderful? It sure is. Do you know what? I'd like to sing a Christmas carol right now. Would you like that? Let's all sing "Silent Night" and the Christmas Tree will lead us. (*ALL SING*) That was just wonderful. And now, I want to show you the picture. Remember what is says? That's right. It says "XMAS." Do you know why the X is there? It stands for Christ. X in Greek is *chi.* In the Greek language it is the first letter in the title, Christ. So when you see "XMAS" you must always think of Jesus Christ. Can you remember that? I bet you can.

Do you know it's time for me to go again. But I'll be back. Yes, I will. I'll be back to be with you, my friend. But until I come back our friend Jesus will always be with you. I hope you and I are friends. And I'll see you tomorrow.

Orders Are Orders

Theme

It doesn't seem to be the practical thing to do — to leave heaven and come to earth to be the Savior of a rebellious people — but that's exactly what the Son of God did. It is something to celebrate.

Summary

Two angels are preparing to announce the birth of baby Jesus but one of them is not happy about the Son of God leaving heaven. When it is explained to the angel that the Son of God left for Love, he understands.

Playing Time	4 minutes
Place	The angel dressing room
Props	A scroll
Costumes	Entirely white costumes; contemporary (no wings and no long robes)
CAST	RANUTE — An angel who is unhappy
	LOM — The angel who is in charge

(TWO ANGELS ARE TALKING)

RANUTE: *(ACTING VERY GLUM AS HE GETS DRESSED)* Glory to God in the highest and Peace to all who receive God's good pleasure.

LOM: Couldn't you at least smile?

RANUTE: *(WITH A FORCED GRIMACE BUT JUST AS MOROSELY)* Glory to God ...

LOM: No. No. You'll just have to do better than that. It's too late to replace you. Brighten up!

RANUTE: Brighten up, he says. I just lost my best friend.

LOM: We all lost Him. We'll all miss Him, won't we?

RANUTE: But I miss Him a lot. It hurt so much to say good-bye to Him. He was a good friend. I'll miss Him. I still don't understand why He had to go.

LOM: I guess I don't understand it fully yet, either. The Father just told us He had to go. We must trust His judgment in this as we have done in all things.

RANUTE: Of course we must trust the Father.

LOM: It hurt the Father, too. Remember, He is His only Son.

RANUTE: I know. To send your only Son away like that — that's why it's so confusing. Why would He do that?

LOM: It had to be done. For them.

RANUTE: They're not worth it. They've proved that on numerous occasions.

LOM: Yes, they are rebellious. It is difficult for us to understand. But the Father loves them very much. You know that.

RANUTE: Yes, I know. And the Father's love means that He will do what must be done for them.

LOM: Yes, even giving up His only Son.

RANUTE: I'm afraid I couldn't do that.

LOM: Of course you couldn't. That's why the Father is the Father and you're an angel who follows orders.

RANUTE: How can I say happy words when I don't feel happy?

LOM: The Father's orders didn't say feel happy. The orders were to say the words He told us to say.

RANUTE: But don't you feel happy when you say. "Glory to God in the highest?"

LOM: Yes, I do.

RANUTE: I usually do, too. But I don't this time. I feel sad.

LOM: You have to go and say the lines as you have been ordered to do.

RANUTE: Okay, I'll go.

LOM: Good.

RANUTE: But I won't like it. Where are we supposed to do this?

LOM: In Bethlehem.

RANUTE: Bethlehem?

LOM: Yeah, you know, Judea.

RANUTE: You're pulling my wing.

LOM: No, really. The orders say Bethlehem, in Judea.

RANUTE: But, that's like going to the middle of the desert. That's just a little town. Two shops and a well, that's it! Why can't we go to a big city like Rome or Athens or at least Jerusalem!

41

LOM: Because the orders say Bethlehem, that's why.

RANUTE: This is ridiculous. Why Bethlehem?

LOM: I don't know. I just know the orders say Bethlehem and I know we're going to be late if we don't hurry.

RANUTE: Okay, okay. I'm coming. Who will hear what we say in this little town of Bethlehem — the sheep?

LOM: No, the shepherds.

RANUTE: Oh, come on — shepherds — come on. In the first place we have to go to the smallest town in a desert and secondly we have to talk to shepherds.

LOM: Those are the orders.

RANUTE: One angel could do it. Let Gabriel do it.

LOM: Let Gabriel do it? I've heard that before.

RANUTE: How many angels does it take to tell a couple of shepherds: "Glory to God — et cetera, et cetera."

LOM: How do you know how many shepherds there will be?

RANUTE: There's only a couple of shepherds in Bethlehem.

LOM: Quit stalling; we're going to be late.

RANUTE: Okay, I'm coming. How many of us are there going to be?

LOM: A multitude.

RANUTE: That's too many for a couple of shepherds — we'll scare them to death — but I can hide in the back.

LOM: Will you hurry!

RANUTE: I'm coming. I'm coming. I don't like it but I'm coming.

LOM: It says that we'll be announcing the birth of the Messiah.

RANUTE: The Messiah? Who's that?

LOM: Only the most important person ever to be born.

RANUTE: Ever?

LOM: The most important ever

RANUTE: If this person is so important why haven't I heard of Him before?

LOM: Because you're just a messenger and if you don't hurry you're going to be demoted.

RANUTE: I am hurrying.

LOM: Do you call this hurrying?

RANUTE: But who is this Messiah?

LOM: I get it!

RANUTE: You get what?

LOM: It says here the Messiah is the Son!

RANUTE: The Son, our friend?

LOM: Correct.

RANUTE: Let me see if I understand this — you say the Son of God, our Creator, is this Messiah who has been born?

LOM: You've got it.

RANUTE: I've got it but I don't understand.

LOM: I don't either.

RANUTE: Why would the Son leave heaven to be the Messiah?

RANUTE AND LOM: Love!

LOM: Right.

RANUTE: Right. Well, come on, what are you waiting for?

The Last Wise Man

Theme

Don't waste your time searching for a false king. Find and worship the real King — Jesus.

Summary

One of the wise men who visited and worshiped Jesus tells the story. (A monologue)

Playing Time	3 minutes
Place	Your church
Props	None
Costumes	Chaldean, first century
Time	Now
Cast	JETUR — a Chaldean

JETUR: (*ENTERS DRESSED IN ROBES APPROPRIATE FOR A MAN OF HIS STATION*) I am afraid I startled some of you. I humbly beg your forgiveness. I intend no harm to you. I only came to explain something to you.

Your minister has graciously offered me a few minutes to speak to you. My name is Jetur ibn Ayub (*HE BOWS*) and I wanted to share with you what I have learned.

It is a long involved story. I saw the Mahdi, uh, you would say *hamasheah*, the Messiah. Here is the way in which it happened.

My father and I are of the Chaldean class — you would call us scientists or men of knowledge. My son also, of course. We had studied for years the stars. My father was much more knowledgable about the positioning of the heavenly bodies than was I. It was because of his knowledge that we knew about the explosion in the western sky.

My father had said that the writings of the ancient ones had prophesied the coming of the Messiah and that His birth would be announced by an announcement in the heavens.

Did not the prophet say that "... a star shall come forth out of Jacob and a scepter shall rise out of Israel" (Numbers 24:17). And again it is written: "Gentiles shall come to your light" (Isaiah 60:3). I was considered a Gentile — an outsider.

My father, my son, and I were not believers. We believed in some higher power. After all, as I said we studied the stars. Who but an intelligent, powerful being could originate such a system?

So, we were searching the western skies for the sign of His coming as the ancient ones had written. The brightness, an explosion of great magnitude in the western sky, lasted for seventy days.

During that time many people saw the sign in the night sky and we discussed with them the possibility that that sign was the awaited sign of the king predicted in the ancient writings.

Some people agreed that it was and, of course, there were some who did not. My father and I decided to find out which were correct. We set out with my son and traveled toward the west.

We traveled to Jericho and then to Jerusalem. We thought, mistakenly, that the king of the Jews would be born in the palace of the Jews — the palace of King Herod. So we went to visit the king.

I want to tell you the truth — I was unwise. Usually I would have been much more clever. But I was in a hurry when we reached Jerusalem and I thought our journey was ended. I didn't think that Herod, the king, was a usurper. So, I asked him: "Where is he who is born king of the Jews?"

To a king who was insecure on his throne he must have thought I asked: "Where is the real king, you impostor?"

King Herod summoned his priests and asked them where the Messiah-king was supposed to be born. The answer was Bethlehem, a little village not far from Jerusalem.

We went there with a promise to Herod that we would return and tell him the location, which we would have done except that we were told by an angel in a dream not to do so.

We found the child and fell down and worshiped Him and presented Him the gifts from our land: gold, frankincense, and myrrh.

That is my story, a simple one, but one you all should remember and maybe you can do likewise. You see we worshiped Him. After all He was a king — *the* king.

Dear friends, do not pass through this life without searching for him diligently. Do not be fooled by a false king. Find the promised one. Find Him, bring Him your gifts, and worship Him.

When

Theme
When was it Jesus realized He was God?

Summary
A couple is talking about Jesus' baptism and wonder when Jesus knew He was Divine.

Playing Time	3 minutes
Place	The home of Sam and Sharon
Props	Newspaper for Sam, Bible for Sam
Costumes	Contemporary
Time	The present
Cast	SAM
	SHARON — his wife

SHARON: (*READING BIBLE*) Sam, what's this passage all about?

SAM: (*READING NEWSPAPER*) What, dear?

SHARON: I said, this passage in the Bible, what's it mean?

SAM: Sharon, I'm trying to read the paper. You're through with what you're doing so you interrupt me, is that it?

SHARON: Since you phrased it so lovingly, yes, that's about it.

SAM: Okay, you got me. Now, what are you reading?

SHARON: The Bible. Ever hear of it?

SAM: No. Is it a new book you bought?

SHARON: Sure.

SAM: Okay, you win. What passage are you talking about?

SHARON: Here it is, where it talks about the baptism of Jesus.

SAM: Okay, let me see it. (*TAKES BIBLE FROM SHARON AND READS*) Yeah, right. What's the problem. Is it about the dove coming down on Him?

SHARON: That was the Holy Spirit. I know that. But what I don't understand is — did Jesus know He was God before His baptism?

SAM: When did Jesus realize He was God?

SHARON: Right.

SAM: That's pretty heavy duty.

SHARON: Well, what do you think? Did He perform miracles when He was a little child? You know, like the story of the little boy, Jesus, forming a bird from clay and then breathing life into it.

SAM: I think we can discount that one. Just a clever story.

SHARON: All right. When, then?

SAM: When did Jesus know He was God? That's the question, right?

SHARON: You know the question. Quit stalling.

SAM: All right. I'll quit stalling. I don't know.

SHARON: Can't we figure it out from the scriptures?

SAM: Okay, okay, let's figure it out. One of the Gospel writers says He was in the Temple when He was twelve. Remember that?

SHARON: Sure. He was asking questions, wasn't He?

SAM: (*LOOKING IN THE BIBLE*) Here it is in Luke. He was learning from the teachers. They were amazed at His understanding and His answers.

SHARON: Isn't that where He said, "I must be doing My Father's work?"

SAM: Yeah, that's what He said.

SHARON: Do you think that was when He realized He was God, when He was twelve, there in the Temple?

SAM: I don't know. He said, "My Father's work," didn't He?

SHARON: Maybe something stirred inside Him at that time to learn more of God. Maybe it was just the beginning of a realization. I remember when I was about that age taking my first trip away from home. My mother put me on a plane and I was a little scared at first and then I realized that the world was so big. I had thought it was just my neighborhood and my school and I found out it was really big with lots of people in it.

SAM: Twelve was the age Hebrew boys started learning the scriptures. He said: "I must be doing My Father's work." That means He must have been thinking about doing His Father's work before that. Therefore, He must have known He was God before that.

SHARON: Now, wait. Jesus was always God, right?

SAM: Right.

SHARON: And was always full of the Holy Spirit, right?

SAM: Right.

SHARON: So, He probably did realize He was God sooner?

SAM: Sooner than twelve?

SHARON: Yeah. He was full of the Holy Spirit. The Holy Spirit would teach Him and also restrain Him.

SAM: What's that got to do with when He knew He was God?

SHARON: Listen to me. If He knew at an early age, younger than twelve, He would have to keep the knowledge to Himself until the right time. The patience of the Holy Spirit would help do that.

SAM: The right time being His baptism. That must have been the sign from God that it was time to begin His ministry. That just might be it.

SHARON: Then we can't know for sure when He knew He was God. Right?

SAM: No, we can't. The Bible doesn't say, so neither can we.

SHARON: But we did learn something.

SAM: We always learn something from searching the scriptures.

SHARON: Stop sounding like a brochure about a church conference.

SAM: Well, we did learn something.

SHARON: Sure. I learned that Jesus was full of the Holy Spirit and therefore He was patient.

SAM: He must have needed patience to wait more than eighteen years to begin a ministry He knew He was called to.

SHARON: I need some of that patience.

SAM: You have it from the Holy Spirit.

SHARON: That's right.

SAM: I know I do.

SHARON: Have patience? You?

SAM: Of course, me. I'm still waiting to read my paper, aren't I?

SHARON: You sure are.

SAM: Right. *(BEGINS READING HIS PAPER)*

SHARON: Sam?

SAM: What is it now?

SHARON: Nothing. Just testing your patience.

SAM: Oh, boy.

Job Placement

Theme
    Working for Jesus, as the disciples learned, takes humility.

Summary
    Two applicants are applying for the position of Spiritual Life Director. Jesus interviews them both. His choice is surprising.

Playing Time	5 minutes
Place	Job Placement Office
Props	None
Costumes	Contemporary
Time	The present
Cast	ELAINE — secretary at Job Placement Office
	LYLE — an applicant
	JANICE — an applicant
	JESUS

(IN A JOB PLACEMENT OFFICE, THERE ARE TWO PEOPLE WAITING TO BE INTERVIEWED)

ELAINE: Now, you two are the applicants for the position of Spiritual Life Coordinator, correct? Good. Have you completed your dexterity test and the basic I.Q. test? *(THE APPLICANTS NOD)* Good. Now, the employer will be along most any minute. So be attentive. When I call your name please step up to the desk and answer His questions promptly and good luck to all of you.

JESUS: *(ENTERS IN MODERN DRESS)* Are the applicants ready?

ELAINE: Yes, they are. Oh, just one question.

JESUS: Yes?

ELAINE: Do you want to talk to the applicants together first or just see them individually?

JESUS: I'll just talk to them individually, thank you, Elaine.

ELAINE: Very good, sir.

JESUS: You may send the first person in.

ELAINE: (*CROSSES TO FIRST APPLICANT*) Mr. Boardman, you're first. (*CROSSES TO JESUS*) The first applicant, sir.

JESUS: You're Lyle Boardman?

LYLE: Yes, sir, that's me.

JESUS: Well, Mr. Boardman, let me see here. You were president of the student organization in your school.

LYLE: That's right. I was elected two years in a row.

JESUS: And how did you obtain that position?

LYLE: Sir?

JESUS: How is it you became president of your student organization?

LYLE: The students voted for me. Well, I campaigned, didn't I? I mean, it was a long and hard process. I was unknown that first year and I went to every campus meeting I could go to and spoke whenever I could and I distributed flyers and shook hands and promised a lot of things to the students.

JESUS: A lot of hard work, right?

LYLE: Right. I built up a fine organization in two years. The second campaign was easy. Our organization worked flawlessly.

JESUS: And what did you do as president?

LYLE: Do? I was the president — the leader of the student body. I campaigned for lower prices in the bookstore. It was because of my efforts that we got a new food service in the student union building. I did a lot of good things for the students. It was good for my organization, too. We learned a lot.

JESUS: Would you classify yourself a leader?

LYLE: Definitely.

JESUS: I see. Did you get a chance to read the job description for this position?

LYLE: I certainly did.

JESUS: I see. And what did you think?

LYLE: Well, sir, I think you need someone to pull your organization together and I think I could easily do that job. I have had experience in my last two positions. It's just a matter of organization. I could do that. I have proven myself a leader and I could certainly be a leader in your organization. If I could be given the freedom to bring in some of my own people I could do some exciting things for you and your organization.

JESUS: I see. Well, thank you very much, Mr. Boardman.

LYLE: Thank you, sir. I'm sure I can do a great job for you. When can I expect to hear from you?

JESUS: Thank you, Mr. Boardman. I'll let you know.

LYLE: In a week? When will you be filling the position?

JESUS: I'll be in touch.

LYLE: Oh, well, then. Okay, well, uh, I'll contact your organization in a week just to see how the recruitment is progressing. *(SHAKING JESUS' HAND)* I have some other possibilities but I think I could really do something for your organization. Good-bye, then. *(CROSSES TO WAITING AREA)*

ELAINE: You're next, Miss Wilton.

JANICE: Oh, yes, thank you. *(CROSSES TO JESUS)*

JESUS: Miss Wilton.

JANICE: Yes, sir.

JESUS: I see you have some qualifications for this job.

JANICE: Well, not exactly. My employment counselor sent me here. I don't mind working, though.

JESUS: Good. Did you get a chance to read the job description?

JANICE: I glanced at it. I didn't really get a chance to study it.

JESUS: I see. You were a member of the committee to feed the poor.

JANICE: It was nice. But all I actually did was fill the paper bags with food and when the people filed past I would get to say a few things to them.

JESUS: Right. And what about that program today? Are you still working with the poor?

JANICE: No, the program was stopped. Lack of funds, I guess.

JESUS: Too bad.

JANICE: Yes, too bad. If you could have seen those people's faces when they picked up their bags — I mean, well, — there was some hope in their faces.

JESUS: And you miss that.

JANICE: I sure do.

JESUS: And how much did that position pay?

JANICE: I was a volunteer, sir.

JESUS: I see. Then you haven't really had a paying position in this area.

JANICE: No, sir. I had a job at the fast food restaurant, that's all.

JESUS: Did you like that job?

JANICE: I cleaned. That's all. But, yes. I liked it. I really did. I helped the people. You know, when they needed something I was there to help them.

JESUS: Dirty work, right?

JANICE: Well, yes, I guess it was, but I didn't mind that part of it. It was being of service that I liked.

JESUS: I see. Well, thank you, Miss Wilton. I'll be in touch.

JANICE: Thank you for your time and consideration, sir. (*CROSSES TO OTHER AREA*)

ELAINE: Sir?

JESUS: Elaine, I think I've made a decision.

ELAINE: So soon?

JESUS: It was easier to choose than I thought. Send in Mr. Boardman, would you, please.

ELAINE: Certainly, sir. Good choice. *(CROSSES TO APPLI-CANTS)* Mr. Boardman, would you go in again, please.

LYLE: *(CROSSES TO JESUS)* Yes, sir?

JESUS: I have made a decision on this position.

LYLE: Great!

JESUS: And I have decided to fill the position with a person other than yourself.

LYLE: What? Are you serious? Not that girl in there. Okay, okay. May I tell you something? I think you're making a mistake. *(EXITS. TO ELAINE)* I really didn't want that job anyway.

JESUS: Would you send in Miss Wilton.

ELAINE: Miss Wilton, would you go in, please. *(JANICE CROSSES TO JESUS)*

JANICE: Sir?

JESUS: I have decided to offer you the position of Spiritual Life Director.

JANICE: Well, I ...

JESUS: I think you can do the work.

JANICE: Well, I've never directed anything in my whole life.

58

JESUS: You enjoy serving. That's what the job is.

JANICE: I'll do my best.

JESUS: I'm sure you will. Thank you. (*JANICE EXITS. TO ELAINE*) I got the job!

ELAINE: (*CROSSES TO JESUS*) Well, you certainly had me fooled. I thought the first applicant would get the job.

JESUS: No, I was looking for something he hadn't even experienced yet.

ELAINE: What was that?

JESUS: Humility.

ELAINE: Well, I'm happy you found the person you wanted. As usual it's a pleasure working with you. Remember, call us when you want to fill some other positions, Jesus.

To Climb A Mountain

Theme:

As the disciples learned, following Jesus is not easy, but it is rewarding.

Summary:

Three climbers seek a guide for the difficult climb up a mountain. They reach the summit and enjoy the rewards of the view. A parable.

Playing Time	4 minutes
Place	A neutral playing area that represents the mountain cabin and mountaintop
Props	None
Costumes	Outerwear for bitter cold
Time	The present
Cast	GUIDE
	GIRL
	BOY
	MAN
	READER

GUIDE: (*SEATED IN HIS MOUNTAIN CABIN. THERE IS A KNOCK AT THE DOOR*) Hmm, late for callers. (*GUIDE OPENS THE DOOR TO REVEAL THREE STRANGERS*) Come in out of the cold. Here, the fire will warm you.

GIRL: Thank you.

BOY: Yes, thanks.

GUIDE: You're welcome. What brings you to my mountain? It's a difficult climb for most people.

MAN: Well, I guess we're no different than most people, but we had to come.

GUIDE: Had to?

MAN: We want to continue.

GUIDE: Up the mountain?

MAN: Yes, that's why we came.

GUIDE: The mountain. Hmm. You think you want to tackle it. Why?

MAN: Because we have to.

GIRL: They say the view is wonderful.

GUIDE: But would you climb it just for the view?

BOY: We know we can do it. We're ready ... we trained for it. Won't you help us?

MAN: Yes, you're the only guide.

GUIDE: There are others.

BOY: But we know you're the only one who can get us there safely.

GUIDE: How do you know that?

MAN: We know the story of your father ...

GIRL: And how he taught you everything about climbing.

GUIDE: Yes, he did. It's true. And you're right, I can take you safely to the top. I just questioned you to learn your motives. The mountain is difficult, but you've taken the first step ... coming to me. And I feel you're ready to move on. We'll get you the right equipment, then we'll begin.

(*DURING THIS NEXT SEQUENCE THE THREE CLIMBERS AND THE GUIDE CAN BE SEEN TOILING UP THE MOUN-TAIN IN MIME*)

READER: In the valley of darkness,
Through the night of gloom,
There is always a pathway to the stars.
When you are enmired ... look up!
When the way is rocky ... take care in walking,
But, walk on.
Don't linger where it is difficult to move onward;
Continue.
You're not alone,
There are others who are walking where you walk,
As many thousands have before you,
Help them when they can no longer help themselves,
But let them continue at the pace that seems best for them.
Don't try to make them conform to your pace,
And you need not conform to theirs,
Just continue.
There are those you'll find who have become so accustomed to the slow pace that they have opted to stay where they only stopped to rest,
Their homes are pitiful shanties made of the same base material in which they were first bogged down,
But you must continue.
For your resting place is on the mountain,
And as difficult as it is to reach,
The more precious for the struggle.
Continue when it seems as if you can't,
Even when you won't ... do!

Your reward will be great.
You can see in all directions from your mountain home,
The air is clear,
The sunlight pure,
And long life to those who claim the prize of the heights.
The prize awaits you,
So, continue.

(*FINALLY THEY REACH THE TOP*)

GUIDE: You were all good climbers and this is your reward. What do you think of that view?

BOY: It is beautiful.

GIRL: And you did get us here safely.

MAN: It was worth it. I could stay here forever.

GUIDE: Rest as long as you want. You deserve it. (*GUIDE BEGINS SONG, OTHERS JOIN IN*)

MEN:
> If any man come after me let him deny himself,
> Pick up his cross and follow me into life eternally.
> Deny himself pick up his cross and daily follow Jesus,
> He is the way, the truth and the life.

WOMEN:
> Hallelujah, Praise the Lord. Let us sing with one accord.
> Hallelujah, King of Kings. Master, Lord of everything.
> Jesus Christ is Lord of all, loving great and small.
> He is the way, the truth and the life.

Be About It

Theme

The beatitudes — they sound good — blessed this and blessed that, but sometimes they sound like rules to follow — and who can?

Summary

A person wanting to make a complaint goes to the complaint department. The complaint concerns the person's church. The churchgoer thinks the beatitudes are rules and she doesn't feel she could live up to them. It is explained to her that they are things you can do and that will please God.

Playing Time	6 minutes
Place	The complaint department in a major department store.
Props	A Bible, a punch bell
Costumes	Merle — a coat and tie
	Georgina — a dress
Time	The present
Cast	GEORGINA — a churchgoer, any gender
	MERLE — a clerk

GEORGINA: (*APPROACHES THE COMPLAINT DEPART-MENT AND RINGS THE BELL FOR SERVICE*) Is anybody there?

MERLE: (*FROM OFF STAGE*) Just a minute.

GEORGINA: (*TO HERSELF*) I've already waited a minute. (*YELLS*) Is this the right department?

MERLE: What department are you looking for?

GEORGINA: Complaints?

MERLE: No, I'm sorry. This is returns. (*ENTERS*) Hello. Complaints? If you have a complaint you must go over there.

GEORGINA: Oh, thank you very much. (*CROSSES OVER THERE*) Hello? Is anybody here?

MERLE: Just a minute.

GEORGINA: (*TO HERSELF*) Now, I've wasted two minutes. (*YELLING*) Is anybody working over here?

MERLE: What department are you looking for?

GEORGINA: You know what department I'm looking for — complaints!

MERLE: You've got the right department.

GEORGINA: Well, is somebody going to help me?

MERLE: (*CROSSING OVER TO HER*) There must not be anybody in right now.

GEORGINA: Well, could you get somebody?

MERLE: They'll be right back, I'm sure.

GEORGINA: I'm on my lunch break.

MERLE: Are you in a hurry?

GEORGINA: Yes, I am. I'm on my lunch break. Could you help me?

MERLE: No. This isn't my department.

GEORGINA: But you're here, aren't you?

MERLE: They don't like us working in other departments.

GEORGINA: Who's going to know? I promise I won't tell.

MERLE: If they find out I'll be in trouble.

GEORGINA: I have a complaint.

MERLE: I'm not so sure you're the kind of person I should trust not to tell on me. You're a complainer.

GEORGINA: I'm not a complainer. I have a legitimate complaint. You needn't worry, it doesn't concern you.

MERLE: It will concern me if I listen to it.

GEORGINA: I have a complaint and I want it handled.

MERLE: Okay, I'll handle it if you promise me one thing.

GEORGINA: One thing? What is it?

MERLE: You won't ever make a complaint about me.

GEORGINA: Don't worry. I doubt if I'll ever see you again.

MERLE: Promise?

GEORGINA: This is ridiculous.

MERLE: Promise, or I won't help you.

GEORGINA: Okay, okay, I promise.

MERLE: Good. Thanks. Now, what's your complaint?

GEORGINA: Well, you see, I go to church.

MERLE: (*WRITING*) That's a complaint?

GEORGINA: There's more. They have all these rules.

MERLE: Uh huh.

GEORGINA: (*BRINGING OUT HER LIST*) And, well, I just can't live up to them all. They've got these rules — you have to be poor — you have to mourn — you have to be meek — you have to be hungry and thirsty — you have to be merciful — you have to pure in heart — you have to be a peacemaker — you have to be persecuted — and you have to rejoice. What do you think of that?

MERLE (*WRITING*) Go - to - church. C-h-u-r-c-h.

GEORGINA: Is that all the farther you are?

MERLE: Don't worry. I've got it all down. Go on.

GEORGINA: That's all there is. Are you sure you have all that?

MERLE: I've got it all.

GEORGINA: Okay, read it back to me so I know you've got it.

MERLE: You really want me to? You're on your lunch break, remember?

GEORGINA: Well, hurry it up, then. Yes, read it all back to me but be quick about it.

MERLE (*HE READS VERY QUICKLY AND DOES AN IMITA-TION OF HER AS HE DOES IT*) Well, you said, "Is anybody

67

there?" Then I said, "Just a minute." Then you said, "I've already waited a minute. (*YELLS*) Is this the right department?" Then I said, "What department are you looking for?" Then you said, "Complaints?" Then I said, "No, I'm sorry. This is returns."

GEORGINA: No, no. Not everything. Not all that. Don't read all that. Just read the rules. Just the rules."

MERLE: Oh, yes, the rules. Let's see. The rules. Ah, yes, here they are — (*READING NORMALLY*) You said, "Well, I just can't live up to them all. They've got rules.

GEORGINA: The rules — get to the rules.

MERLE: Sure, sure. Hey, you sure are touchy.

GEORGINA: It's my lunch hour. I'm in a hurry.

MERLE: I forgot. You're in a hurry. (*READING FAST AGAIN*) You said, "— you have to be poor — you have to mourn — you have to be meek — you have to be hungry and thirsty — you have to be merciful — you have to be pure in heart — you have to be a peacemaker — you have to be persecuted — and you have to rejoice."

GEORGINA: I guess you did get it all down.

MERLE: Good. Do you feel any better?

GEORGINA: What do you mean, do I feel any better?

MERLE: Since you told me these things — do you feel better about it?

GEORGINA: No, of course I don't feel any better. How could I feel better? I've just told you my complaints. Nothing has been done about them yet.

MERLE: I know that but sometimes people feel better just telling someone else.

GEORGINA: Well, I don't. I want something to be done about the situation.

MERLE: Is there anything you can do to improve the situation?

GEORGINA: What are you talking about?

MERLE: Is there anything you can do in your church to improve ...

GEORGINA: You don't understand. I'm not here for psychological counseling. I came to the complaint department because I have some complaints about my church.

MERLE: I understand that often if we change, the situation seems to improve.

GEORGINA: Get back to my church.

MERLE: Right. Now, is there any possibility that you misinterpreted these "rules"?

GEORGINA: No! Of course not. I copied them down as the preacher was discussing them.

MERLE: And where did he get them?

GEORGINA: Well, how should I know? He made them up, I guess.

MERLE: Not necessarily. Maybe he had some reference work. I know that preachers often cite the Bible when they preach. Did he use the Bible when he was talking about these rules?

GEORGINA: Well, yes.

MERLE: Good, good. Now, we're getting somewhere. (*SEARCHING FOR A BIBLE*) A Bible, a Bible. Let's see. (*FINDING ONE*) Here we are.

GEORGINA: I don't see what this has to do with my complaint about the church.

MERLE: Just wait a minute.

GEORGINA: I've already waited five minutes.

MERLE: Here it is in Matthew's Gospel. The heading says it's called the Beatitudes.

GEORGINA: What's that mean?

MERLE: I don't know but you copied it down wrong. It says here the word "blessed" in front of all the rules.

GEORGINA: What does that mean?

MERLE: Well, I suppose "blessed" means blessed! In other words what you thought were rules set down by your church aren't rules at all.

GEORGINA: They're not?

MERLE: Not if you're blessed if you do them. They must be ways you as a Christian can please your God.

GEORGINA: Well, how about that. In other words I don't have to be these things, but I can do them and if I do them I'm "blessed" if I do.

MERLE: That must be it.

GEORGINA: Well, I do feel better now.

70

MERLE: Good.

GEORGINA: It's like getting a load off my back.

MERLE: Do you want this?

GEORGINA: The Bible?

MERLE: I just found it back here. You can have it. I would think if you have questions about what your church teaches you would want to check this to make sure they were true.

GEORGINA: No, you keep it. I'm going to buy one of my own. Does your store sell Bibles?

MERLE: Of course they do. Right over there.

GEORGINA (*CROSSES OVER THERE*) Good. I'll just buy one. Is anybody here?

MERLE: Just a minute.

GEORGINA: (*TO HERSELF*) I've already waited ten minutes. Is this the right department?

MERLE: What department are you looking for?

GEORGINA: You know what department I'm looking for — Bibles!

MERLE: That's the right department.

GEORGINA: Will you help me, please?

MERLE: You know I can't help you. They don't like ...

GEORGINA: Never mind. I've used all my lunch break. My lunch break! Oh, dear! I'm late.

71

MERLE: Are you angry?

GEORGINA: Of course I'm angry! You made me miss my entire lunch break. Why won't you help me? I want to see the manager.

MERLE: You know why I can't help you. They don't like it ...

GEORGINA: I want the manager! I want the manager!

MERLE: I'll call the manager but what are you going to do?

GEORGINA: I have a complaint.

MERLE: I knew it. I shouldn't have trusted you. You're a complainer.

GEORGINA: (*EXITING*) Oh, great. I missed my lunch hour for this.

MERLE: (*FOLLOWING HER OUT*) And you promised, too.

You And The Law

Theme

There is a relationship between being guilty, the law, and forgiveness. But how does it really operate?

Summary

Dave, an eighteen year old, has had an accident with the family car. It's not a horrible accident but the other car was a police car. Marge, Dave's mom, is understandably angry and grounds her son. Their discussion of the punishment reveals the nature of forgiveness.

Playing Time	4 minutes
Setting	Their home
Props	None
Costumes	Casual, appropriate for the characters
Time	The present
Cast	MARGE — a middle-aged woman
	DAVE — her son

MARGE: (*ENTERS, FOLLOWING DAVE*) You're grounded!

DAVE: But, Mom, I ...

MARGE: I suppose you're going to tell me you didn't hit that car.

DAVE: I had an accident. I couldn't help it. It was an accident. He was stopped right in the middle of the street and I plowed right into him. It was an accident. I couldn't help it. That's why they call them accidents, because you can't help ...

MARGE: You wouldn't have had the accident if you would have been paying attention.

DAVE: I was paying attention.

MARGE: Paying attention to what? To what?

DAVE: Well, he shouldn't have stopped in front of me like that.

MARGE: What were you doing when you hit that car?

DAVE: What was he doing right in the middle of the street?

MARGE: Why didn't you see him stop? What were you looking at?

DAVE: Possibly, just for a moment, mind you, my attention could have been momentarily diverted.

MARGE: Aha! Just for a moment, eh?

DAVE: The smallest of possible moments. A minuscule, fleeting glance in another direction.

MARGE: At what? What were you looking at?

DAVE: Girls.

MARGE: Girls? I knew it. Girls!

DAVE: Some girls were walking down the street. I took a look.

MARGE: And plowed into a car.

DAVE: Girls, Mom. I'm eighteen. I can't help it. I look at girls.

MARGE: Okay, you look at girls. But did you have to plow into a car while you were looking? Of all the people out there you had to hit a policeman.

DAVE: He was the only one dumb enough to be sitting in the middle of the street.

MARGE: While you were ogling the girls.

DAVE: Don't say "ogling." It sounds so dirty — "ogling."

MARGE: It is dirty. I meant it to sound that way. You were ogling.

DAVE: Okay. Put it on my criminal record — "David Wilson, age 18, convicted of two counts of ogling nubile females."

MARGE: That does sound dirty.

DAVE: Well, it wasn't dirty. It was an accident.

MARGE: This is your first brush with the law.

DAVE: "Brush with the law." What does that mean?

MARGE: It means that you'll probably end up leading a life of crime.

DAVE: Mom, I had an accident. I'm not a criminal.

MARGE: It all has to start somewhere — a "little" accident, then you'll be smoking marijuana, then the harder stuff, and then robbing banks, and then it's death row.

DAVE: Oh, for Pete's sake. I had an accident. If I have criminal tendencies they are probably inherited.

MARGE: Don't bring your father's family into this.

DAVE: I imagine the punishment that will be meted out to me will more than change my life for the good. Grounded! I'm eighteen!

MARGE: If you're old enough to drive our only car into that policeman's rear end you're old enough to deal with the consequences.

DAVE: You're a Christian. What would Jesus have to say about this punishment?

MARGE: Jesus, I'm sure, agrees with me.

DAVE: But the Bible says that Jesus came to abolish the law, so I'm free in Jesus.

MARGE: No so fast, my misinformed, biblical scholar. Jesus came to fulfill the law, not to abolish it.

DAVE: I'll bet Jesus never grounded any of the disciples.

MARGE: Maybe He should have.

DAVE: Who?

MARGE: Judas.

DAVE: Okay. Where's the Christian compassion?

MARGE: It comes after the Christian justice.

DAVE: I need the compassion first.

MARGE: First, you get justice. You're grounded.

DAVE: Okay, I'm grounded. Look, Mom, I'm sorry.

MARGE: Sorry?

DAVE: Sorry, have you heard of it?

MARGE: Not from you. So, you're sorry. What about the damages?

DAVE: I'll pay the damages. I work, you know.

MARGE: You're saving for your education.

DAVE: I think I just got one.

MARGE: Yes, I guess you did.

DAVE: *(HUGGING MARGE)* Well, am I forgiven?

MARGE: Of course you are. Now, stay out of my way. I've got work to do.

DAVE: Okay, Mom, I'll see ya. *(BEGINNING TO EXIT)*

MARGE: See ya. Hey! Wait! Where are you going?

DAVE: Out.

MARGE: Okay, don't be late. *(DAVE EXITS)* You're grounded. Oh, well. I wonder sometimes if I should have taught him about forgiveness.

Robin Hood?

Theme

Jesus, when He taught the kingdom truths in His Sermon on the Mount, turned the values of the world upside down.

Summary

Robin Hood is questioned about his practice of stealing and decides to quit.

Playing Time	6 minutes
Costumes	Legendary
Props	Robin — an apple with an arrow through it
Place	Sherwood Forest
Time	The time of legends
Cast	ROBIN HOOD
	FRIAR TUCK
	LITTLE JOHN

ROBIN HOOD: (*ENTERS CARRYING AN APPLE WITH AN ARROW PIERCING IT*) Ho, there.

LITTLE JOHN: (*TAKES APPLE AND BEGINS TO EAT IT*) Foresooth! What sight from yonder verdant wood do I see? Robin, the most wanted outlaw entereth having killed an apple. The hunted becomes the hunter, indeed. Didst thou sneakily track its tender trail through the rooky wood, catching it napping or didst thou warily sneaketh upon it whilst it paused, mayhap drinking its fill from a placid pool? Ah, alas much more, wouldst I be haply viewing a fine antlered specimen from the King's own herd.

ROBIN: Shuteth thy overstuffed mouth, John Little, thou louty layabout! Whilst I risketh my life amongst the wild furzy wood thou resteth here safe by thy fire.

JOHN: It doth thee no good, Sir Hoodlum, to rail upon my poor station. He who guardeth is worth the equal of he who hunteth — especially if he who hunteth, hunteth for apples.

ROBIN: If needs thee to know my work, John, and I think not that thou needeth, I shooteth the apple for practice solely. (*GRABBING THE APPLE BACK FROM JOHN*)

JOHN: Well, seedlings and blossoms, Robin, what dost thou supposeth me to eat?

ROBIN: Not my apple, surely, for by thy bearded grandmother I chooseth an apple that was the home of a worm.

JOHN: Yuketh! What then? There hath been this long and dreary fortnight no meat of which to speaketh.

ROBIN: Remembereth thou not the sumptuous meal that was luxuriously laid before us only yesterday?

JOHN: I remembereth it well, Robin, but I remembereth that it consisteth of the bean of soy — faux hamburger.

ROBIN: Well, fee fie faux foo and fow to thou. Faux, indeed. Knowest not, friend John, that I ordereth that fare ...

JOHN: Faux fare.

ROBIN: That I ordereth that fare full knowing the contents thereof? In truth I doeth it for thine own sake.

JOHN: Sayeth not so, Robin?

ROBIN: In truth I sayeth. Knoweth thee not that I knoweth all concerning nutrition?

JOHN: Huh?

ROBIN: Thou lamest of brains, nutrition is something that havest to do with what thou eatest.

JOHN: Oh, yeah.

ROBIN: The bean of soy is good for thy digestion.

JOHN: Huh?

ROBIN: Never thee mind, dear friend John. The explaining of it would take too long. And the understanding, never.

FRIAR TUCK: (*ENTERS*) Hail, Robin.

ROBIN: And a hi-thee-well to thee, fair companion, this day, Friar.

JOHN: Thou art well met, Friar Tuck. Didst thou see any game about?

FRIAR: Nary a hare. (*GRABBING APPLE FROM ROBIN AND BITING INTO IT*) Yuketh!

JOHN: What couldst be the problem?

FRIAR: I think, dear friends, that the dearth of game must be causeth by a lack of animals.

ROBIN: Yea, verily. Although the truth of which you speak soundeth tinny to my ear.

JOHN: All gone? All the animals vanisheth?

ROBIN: What will we do? We cannot, in all truth, live longer in this tranquil glade without game to eat.

FRIAR: I supposeth we will have needs to revert to our old ways.

JOHN: Nay, tell me not the truth.

ROBIN: Dost thou mean ... ?

FRIAR: Yea, and verily. We must needs henceforth work for our living.

ROBIN: Drat! That it cometh to this.

JOHN: Do I read your meaning thus — we must needs be the farmers that raiseth the bean of soy?

FRIAR: Ah, tis true. Tis true. We must, by the sweat of our brow, till the unkind earth.

ROBIN: But we are unused to such labor. We shall falter in the doing of it.

FRIAR: And why are thou so unused to work, Robin?

ROBIN: Why, thou knowest truly, good Friar. I was trained to rob and steal, of course. Thou knowest this?

JOHN: Yea and verily. It is what we do best, is it not?

FRIAR: It is a truth, surely. It is what we do best, but I thinkest to myself that it is not the will of Almighty God, who rulest the vast universe.

ROBIN: But, kind Friar, and dearest friend, Almighty God, who rules our lives, cannot intend for us to allow the mean Sheriff to continue stealing from the poor.

FRIAR: Hast thou tried prayer, Robin?

JOHN: Art thou of a serious nature whenst thou suggesteth that?

FRIAR: I am, verily.

ROBIN: But how could prayer help our situation? We are men of action.

FRIAR: I fully understand your situation.

JOHN: And this play is supposed to be a play of action. I ain't seen nary a battle yet.

FRIAR: Dear friend, duck your sweaty head in a pail of patience.

JOHN: Why, I ought to ... (*HE GRABS FOR THE FRIAR*)

ROBIN: Be resourceful with thine energy, John. Let Tuck say his say. Continue. I wouldest knoweth more of this prayer.

FRIAR: Firstly, the Bible teaches us to pray for those who rule over us.

JOHN: The Bible? When did he learn to readeth?

ROBIN: Never thee mind.

FRIAR: I cannot readeth, of course, but I heardeth the Abbot readeth the Bible once.

JOHN: Once!

ROBIN: Shhh-eth!

FRIAR: Secondly, we knoweth that stealing is against the law.

JOHN: Telleth that to King John. He's been stealing from the people since his incarnation.

ROBIN: Not "incarnation," thou denseth of dunces. The word you want is "incarceration." Since the king's incarceration.

FRIAR: Not "incarceration" or "incarnation." Thou misseth the mark. The word thou searchest for is "coronation." Dost thou not remember we witnesseth King John's coronation? He was coronated by a coroner.

ROBIN: Thy learning astoundeth me.

JOHN: Yea, but my pointeth is: the King stealeth so why shouldn't we?

ROBIN: John graspeth upon a grain of truth, thou must admiteth, Tuck.

FRIAR: One man's sin needeth not be reason for another's sin.

JOHN: Zounds, that Abbot readeth a long passage.

FRIAR: Watcheth thy mouth. But thou art correct. Indeed the Abbot did readeth a long passage.

JOHN: But the King is our enemy. We have to fighteth him. I itcheth for a good fight.

ROBIN: Thy itcheth all the time, John.

FRIAR: The Bible teacheth us to loveth our enemies.

ROBIN: So, thou art saying that we shouldest stealeth no more and loveth our enemies.

FRIAR: And honoreth the king.

JOHN: To whom no honoreth is due.

FRIAR: Honoreth is due God. We must allowest God to dealeth with the King.

JOHN: I geteth it. We cannot be God. I will doeth it. I will become a laborer and no longer stealeth anything.

FRIAR: A noble vow, John.

ROBIN: I geteth it too, but I will never till the stubborn earth. I think I will starteth an industry of some sort.

JOHN: Huh?

FRIAR: He speaketh in riddles.

JOHN: Huh?

ROBIN: I will manufactureth something. Something the populace will have need of.

JOHN: Huh?

FRIAR: What will you maketh, Robin?

ROBIN: Money, I hopeth.

JOHN: I understoodeth that!

FRIAR: No, I meaneth, what will you manufacture for the populace to buy?

ROBIN: I thinketh I will maketh home security systems.

FRIAR AND JOHN: HUH?!

The Tooth Fairy

Theme

People retaliate for a wrong done to them and think it is right. Jesus said, "Don't pay back evil for evil."

Summary

The Tooth Fairy visits Albert to pay him "tooth for tooth." He knocked out someone's tooth so he will now have his knocked out.

Playing Time	7 minutes
Place	A neutral playing area that represents Albert's home
Props	Pistol
Costumes	Albert — pajamas
	The Tooth Fairy — overalls
Time	The present
Cast	ALBERT — a bully
	THE TOOTH FAIRY — a big brute

THE TOOTH FAIRY: (*CALLING SOFTLY TO ALBERT WHO IS ASLEEP*) Albert. Albert. Albert. (*YELLING*) Albert!

ALBERT: (*HE HAS A BLACK EYE*) What? How dare you. Why I ought to ... (*HE GRABS A PISTOL FROM UNDER THE PILLOW AND POINTS IT AT THE TOOTH FAIRY*)

THE TOOTH FAIRY: (*GRABBING ALBERT AND RESTRAIN-ING HIM*) Just calm down. I'm here to bring you a present.

85

ALBERT: A present? Well, this is a strange way to deliver a present, in the middle of the night, sneaking into a man's bedroom.

THE TOOTH FAIRY: I came in through the window.

ALBERT: You came in through the window? You're a burglar.

THE TOOTH FAIRY: No, I am not a burglar. Have you ever heard of any burglars waking up their victims?

ALBERT: Well, no, I can't say that I have. For that matter you could have gotten my name from the phone book.

THE TOOTH FAIRY: Well, I didn't.

ALBERT: You didn't?

THE TOOTH FAIRY: Why would I wake you up to rob you?

ALBERT: I don't know. Why did you?

THE TOOTH FAIRY: I'm not going to rob you. I'm here to deliver my present.

ALBERT: Did the guys at the office dream this up?

THE TOOTH FAIRY: No.

ALBERT: No? Well, who did then?

THE TOOTH FAIRY: I represent the law.

ALBERT: The law?

THE TOOTH FAIRY: Why do you have to repeat everything I say? Do you do that all the time?

ALBERT: All the time? No, I don't think so. Why?

THE TOOTH FAIRY: Because it irritates me.

ALBERT: It irritates you?

THE TOOTH FAIRY: YES IT DOES! STOP IT! This would be a lot easier if you just listen and then I can give you the present and leave.

ALBERT: All right, but why not let me go and we can talk, I mean, I can listen and you can talk.

THE TOOTH FAIRY: That's better. But you have to drop the gun first.

ALBERT: Drop the gun first? I will not.

THE TOOTH FAIRY: I can force you to drop it.

ALBERT: You think you can force me to drop it? Oh, yeah?

THE TOOTH FAIRY: Yeah. You're repeating me again. I don't like that, remember? I ought to make you drop it just because I don't like you repeating me all the time.

ALBERT: You're a bully.

THE TOOTH FAIRY: In your situation you better call me Mr. Bully. Now drop the gun! (*GRABBING ALBERT AND FORC-ING HIM*)

ALBERT: I will not. I have to protect myself against bullies like you.

THE TOOTH FAIRY: Drop it. (*THERE IS A BRIEF STRUG-GLE BUT ALBERT DROPS THE GUN*) There, that's better.

87

ALBERT: You almost broke my arm.

THE TOOTH FAIRY: You had a gun. What would you have done if I would have let you go?

ALBERT: I would have made you get out of my house.

THE TOOTH FAIRY: I wouldn't have gone.

ALBERT: Oh, yes you would. I would have the gun.

THE TOOTH FAIRY: But you don't have it now. I do. Now, let's talk so I can give you the present.

ALBERT: Hurry up and give it to me.

THE TOOTH FAIRY: No. We're going to talk first.

ALBERT: I remember. Go ahead.

THE TOOTH FAIRY: Good. Now, remember last Friday when you were out drinking and ...

ALBERT: I was relaxing after work. The boys in the office always stop for one, Friday after work.

THE TOOTH FAIRY: Don't interrupt. Listen.

ALBERT: Okay, okay. We just had a few.

THE TOOTH FAIRY: A few too many for you. You got into a pretty big argument with Lou Winger.

ALBERT: Ah, that stupid ...

THE TOOTH FAIRY: (*MOTIONS FOR SILENCE*) Now, as I was saying, you got into an argument and then you started fighting.

ALBERT: Say, how do you know all this?

THE TOOTH FAIRY: I represent the law.

ALBERT: You do, huh. And Lou Winger is pressing charges, is that it?

THE TOOTH FAIRY: No. Oh, no. Not at all. One of my friends is visiting Lou tonight. He's getting a present, too.

ALBERT: A present? That louse? Why would anyone give him a present?

THE TOOTH FAIRY: The law requires it.

ALBERT: The law, huh? Well, Lou got the worst of the fight. I knocked out his tooth.

THE TOOTH FAIRY: Yes, I know. And he gave you that black eye.

ALBERT: That's right. Boy, I'm going to get him good.

THE TOOTH FAIRY: You're not going to continue the violence, are you? Didn't you ever hear about turning the other cheek?

ALBERT: Turning the other cheek? Are you kidding? Are you from my sister's church? She's preaching that goody-goody stuff to me all the time. "Jesus said, 'Turn the other cheek.' " Rubbish! I was just protecting myself. A man's got a right to protect himself, doesn't he? "An eye for an eye," I say.

THE TOOTH FAIRY: That's a fair law.

ALBERT: Sure.

THE TOOTH FAIRY: But what if you shoot someone when you're in a fit of rage like last Friday?

89

ALBERT: Shoot Lou? Boy, if I would've had this gun ...

THE TOOTH FAIRY: That's what I thought. It's a good thing I was sent to give you my present.

ALBERT: Sent? Sent by whom?

THE TOOTH FAIRY: I already told you. I represent the law.

ALBERT: Good. Then you're fair. The law is fair, isn't it?

THE TOOTH FAIRY: Oh, yes. Quite impartial and fair — *lex talionis.*

ALBERT: Good. Well, get on with it. Wait. Who is Lex what's-his-name?

THE TOOTH FAIRY: *Lex talionis,* it means the law of retaliation. I represent that law.

ALBERT: Just get on with it. Where is my present?

THE TOOTH FAIRY: You don't want to protest?

ALBERT: Why should I protest. I trust the law. I live by the law.

THE TOOTH FAIRY: Glad to hear it. Most people are such cowards when they get their present.

ALBERT: I'm not a coward. I knocked out Lou Winger's tooth, didn't I?

THE TOOTH FAIRY: You surely did. And he blackened your eye.

ALBERT: It still hurts, too.

THE TOOTH FAIRY: A friend of mine is returning the favor, right about now.

ALBERT: Do you mean someone is punching Lou in the eye right now?

THE TOOTH FAIRY: Right about now, yes. We were sent out about the same time.

ALBERT: (*LAUGHING*) Oh, that's great. Lou gets a black eye and I get a present. That's great.

THE TOOTH FAIRY: Oh, you are good sport.

ALBERT: Sure, why not. I'm ready, now. How about giving me my present.

THE TOOTH FAIRY: All right. (*HE CLOSES IN ON ALBERT AND DRAWS HIS ARM BACK AS IF TO SOCK HIM IN THE JAW*)

ALBERT: Hey, what are you doing? Who are you anyway?

THE TOOTH FAIRY: My friends call me "The Tooth Fairy!" (*ALBERT RUNS AWAY. THE TOOTH FAIRY RUNS OUT AFTER HIM*)

Servant And Two Masters

Theme

We make a choice whom we will serve — God or the world.

Summary

This vignette is like the *Comeddia dell Arte* of sixteenth century, Italy. It is light and fun and the costumes are extravagant. Nickolo is the servant of two masters, the lovable Adonatino and the miserly Mammonitees. He finds he must make a choice to serve one or the other.

Playing Time	5 minutes
Place	The stage of the *Comeddia dell Arte*
Props	Ledger, stool, bag of gold
Costumes	The costumes of *Comeddia del Arte*
Time	The sixteenth century, Italy
Cast	NICKOLO — the servant
	ADONATINO — good master
	MAMMONITEES — evil master
	WIDOW

NICKOLO: (*A SERVANT AND A VERY CLEVER FELLOW. HE ADDRESSES THE AUDIENCE*) I am a fellow most worthy of praising, at least among you into whose hearts I'm gazing.

Doubly attuned to work am I, but from one master to the other I fly. (*ADONATINO ENTERS AND STANDS*) Here, Adonatino, much loved and adored, to all unselfish and to all in accord. (*MAMMONITEES ENTERS AND STANDS OPPOSITE ADONATINO*) And here, Mammonitees, all grouchy and growl, He takes what is his and repays with a scowl.

Wealth in abundance is near both their hands, and palaces of beauty rest on their lands.

Mammonitees, flinty gray with heart as cold, beckons my presence as if to scold.

MAMMONITEES: Nickolo, you lazy, louting fool, bring me my ledgers. Where is my stool? (*NICKOLO RUSHES ABOUT EXECUTING HIS MASTER'S WILL, GIVING HIM HIS LEDGER AND HIS STOOL JUST BEFORE MAMMONITEES HITS THE FLOOR*)

NICKOLO: Adonatino, good and with heart of gold, calls me to him with virtues manifold.

ADONATINO: Nickolo, come to me and you will be blest, I wish to share my wealth with the rest. (*NICKOLO RUSHES TO ADONATINO AND RECEIVES A BAG OF GOLD TO GIVE TO OTHERS*)

NICKOLO: So, here is the problem that lays in my lap, I have double duty but therein lies a trap. For my good master on the South side resides, and he with greed on the North abides. So, as I'm bid, I run and scurry, hither and back always with a hurry. And neither to the other am I known, so that in each of their minds, think me their own.

MAMMONITEES: Nickolo, go and collect this rent! From the widow you snatch it ere on bread it's spent. (*NICKOLO SCURRIES TO RUN HIS ERRAND SNATCHING MONEY FROM A WIDOW*)

ADONATINO: Take this bread, my man, to a woman I know. Direst of need faces her by my trow. (*NICKOLO TAKES BREAD TO THE SAME WIDOW*)

NICKOLO: (*EXHAUSTED*) Not only is this business wearing me thin, I think I am on the brink of sin. If by doing the bidding of one, I negate the bad that the other has done. Then, good has no chance to win, but just stay even and therein lies the sin.

Good must abound says God's Book to me, and how can it happen?

ADONATINO: You are the key!

NICKOLO: I? Change this business? How can this come about?

ADONATINO: You must choose which to serve and which lifestyle to tout. When duty calls you must choose the right, then, good will increase and God will win the fight.

NICKOLO: Ah, but 'tis easier said than done, my Lord, when worries tell me they're aboard. I also have a wife and children to feed, and how can I afford the family steed?

ADONATINO: Take no thought for what you shall eat, or the shoes for the children's feet. Fret not for what you will drink, for to you heaven is on the brink.

NICKOLO: What do I do when the wolf is knocking?

ADONATINO: Trust in God to fill your stocking. Look at the birds who in the air do fly, do not they eat and drink with no need to buy? And the flowers, so wondrous in their beauty? Are they not splendid without worry or duty? God will care for you in all your need, (*AS HE HELPS NICKOLO INTO A FINE JACKET*) And as for the future you will take no heed. (*HE GIVES NICKOLO A BAG OF MONEY*)

NICKOLO: Then, in faith, I will trust Him who sustains, and will serve Him with all my life's gains.

ADONATINO: And when money calls what will you do?

MAMMONITEES: Nickolo!

NICKOLO: Quit his service and to you be true.

ADONATINO: So, from your experience what have you gained?

NICKOLO: This much — God has on me goodness rained. Henceforth from this day only Him will I trust. My future and fortune He will add as He must. (*ALL BOW AND EXIT*)

A Light Verse

Theme

Does knowing Jesus change a person's life?

Summary

Two Christians are busy learning Bible verses and ignore Ollie, who is slow. They learn patience and kindness from the one they have hurt.

Playing Time	5 minutes
Place	A work place
Props	Two coffee cups
Costumes	Contemporary, casual
Time	The present
Cast	GREG
	MARK — his friend
	OLLIE

GREG: (*ENTERING WITH TWO COFFEE CUPS*) Well, here's your coffee, just the way you like it, double cream and no sugar. Are you ready for this week's verse? I don't mean to lose again.

MARK: Well, I'm going to win again.

GREG: Here comes Ollie. C'mon, Ollie.

MARK: That guy is so slow. Why do we have to have him along? We only have a ten-minute break, you know.

GREG: I know, but think of him as a ministry. C'mon, Ollie. You're the official judge.

OLLIE: (*ARRIVING, FINALLY*) Yup.

MARK: You ready?

GREG: You go first.

MARK: No, you.

GREG: Why should I go first?

MARK: You don't know it, do you?

GREG: Of course I know it.

MARK: Let's do it. Ollie, you ready?

OLLIE: Yup. Ready?

MARK AND GREG: Ready!

OLLIE: Ready. Set. Go!

MARK AND GREG: (*IT IS A CONTEST OF MEMORIZATION DONE QUITE FAST*) And while He was praying, the appearance of His face became different, and His clothing became white and gleaming. And behold, two men were talking with Him; and they were Moses and Elijah.

MARK: You missed a word.

GREG: I did not.

MARK: You did.

GREG: Which word?

MARK: I don't know. But, you missed one.

GREG: I didn't.

MARK: You did.

GREG: You don't know the word.

MARK: No. I don't.

GREG: Well, then.

MARK: Ollie, did he miss a word or not?

OLLIE: Yup, you missed a word, Greg.

GREG: What word?

OLLIE: "Gleaming."

MARK: "Gleaming," that was it. "Gleaming." You owe me a coffee. I win again. I guess I'm the all-time champion. Next week I plan to win again.

GREG: We'll see.

OLLIE: "Gleaming."

MARK: That was the word.

GREG: Will you guys cut it out. I admit I lost.

OLLIE: What does it mean?

MARK: "Gleaming." Uh. (*PAUSE. MARK AND GREG THINK. OLLIE LOOKS FROM ONE TO THE OTHER*)

GREG: It means ... uh, kinda shiny-like, you know.

MARK: Yeah, shiny-like.

OLLIE: Jesus' clothes were all shiny-like? Why?

GREG: Why? I don't know. Because He was God, I guess.

MARK: Yeah, He was not only a man, He was God too, don't forget.

OLLIE: Oh, I know that. But why didn't He shine all the time, then?

MARK: I don't know. Maybe God the Father didn't want Him to.

OLLIE: Oh.

GREG: What's the scripture for next week?

OLLIE: "His face changed."

MARK: Will you get off it. We're thinking about next week already.

OLLIE: The verse says, "His face changed."

MARK AND GREG: "And while He was praying the appearance of His face became different ..."

OLLIE: How?

GREG: I wish you wouldn't ask so many questions, Ollie. We're memorizing Bible verses, here, you know. This is serious and we don't like you asking questions that are unimportant.

OLLIE: I just wanted to know how His face changed. Was it like this? (*HE MAKES A FACE AND THEN ANOTHER*) Or like this?

MARK: Stop that. That's no way to talk about Jesus. Of course He didn't make weird faces.

OLLIE: Well, how, then? (*PAUSE. GREG AND MARK THINK. OLLIE LOOKS FROM ONE TO THE OTHER*)

GREG: How did His face change? Uh ... I don't know. It just changed. You just have to accept some things in the Bible without questioning them.

OLLIE: Okay. Why?

MARK: Why, what?

OLLIE: Why did His face change?

GREG: Ollie, I just told you ...

OLLIE: I know, but you said that for "how," now I'm asking "why."

GREG: Oh, yeah, why.

OLLIE: Yup, why? (*PAUSE. GREG AND MARK THINK. OLLIE LOOKS FROM ONE TO THE OTHER*)

MARK: Why? Uh ... I don't know. I guess God the Father wanted it to change.

OLLIE: Greg, you always told me that Jesus never changed.

GREG: Yes, I told you that, but this is different.

OLLIE: Different, how?

GREG: Well, let's see. Jesus will never change who He really is, inside, but His outer appearance could look different.

OLLIE: Oh.

MARK: Now that that is settled, what *is* the verse for next week?

OLLIE: So what?

MARK: Ollie, what do you mean, so what? I'm getting a little tired of you interrupting.

OLLIE: Sorry, but I was just thinking, so what if Jesus' clothes were all shiny-like and His face changed ... so what does that mean to me?

MARK: (*TO GREG*) You talk to him. I can't.

GREG: Now, listen, Ollie ...

OLLIE: I was thinking. Maybe Jesus let God shine through Him all the time and this time other people saw it. And that would change anyone's face. That must be it. Thanks, guys, for letting me be a part of your Bible study. (*HE STARTS TO EXIT*) I love you both. Bye. (*HE EXITS*)

MARK: Hey, let's pray. I have some repenting to do.

Fasting

Theme

Is it possible for the average Christian to fast or is it just for the super spiritual saint? And why do we fast?

Summary

Two people talk about their struggle to fast as a preparation for Easter. They learn that they can be strengthened in the process.

Playing Time	3 minutes
Place	Anywhere
Props	None
Costumes	Contemporary, casual
Time	The present
Cast	RON — a struggler
	JAN — another one

RON: Hey, are you still hungry? I am.

JAN: It was a good dinner. But, please, don't talk about dessert.

RON: I can't help it. That's all I think about.

JAN: Me too. That's why I told you not to talk about it.

RON: C'mon, wouldn't a great piece of cheesecake with blueberry topping taste really good right about now?

JAN: Well, of course it would. Dinner was great and it would be nice to top it off with a nice dessert.

RON: There, you see. Let's forget the fast and go get some dessert — fast!

JAN: "Get thee behind me, Satan."

RON: Okay. I can prove that I have a strong will. I'll just talk about something else. Let's see. Oh, did you know that that new building downtown is renting space now?

JAN: It's not finished.

RON: Of course, but the building is really nice and we need to move the office. The lease rates are really low right now.

JAN: Well, let's go look at it sometime.

RON: Great, how about this afternoon? We could stop at that yogurt place and get a cone.

JAN: Ron!

RON: I'm sorry. I did it again, didn't I?

JAN: Don't worry about it. If you hadn't mentioned dessert I probably would have.

RON: This fasting is really getting to me. Of all the things we decided to do, fasting is the worst. I just can't do it. Let's forget the whole thing and go eat dessert.

JAN: No, no. We both thought the Lord was telling us to fast for Lent.

RON: But, I can't do it. All day yesterday I thought about dessert. And the day before that was worse.

JAN: I know. I know. Isn't it strange, I mean, who would think that the Lord God, Creator of the universe, would care if we ate a little itty bitty piece of cherry pie or not?

RON: Do you think He cares? How can whether we eat a dessert after dinner matter to someone who is negotiating the umpteen zillionth turn of this earth around the sun?

JAN: What's fasting all about then?

RON: Why are we hurting ourselves, denying ourselves?

JAN: I really don't know. Everyone else is doing it. The pastor asked us to fast. He asked the entire church.

RON: I know, but why are we doing it? No one is going to know whether we do or not, right?

JAN: Right. Of course no one will know if we fast or not. Probably no one would care, but wouldn't God know?

RON: Of course God knows. Of course He does. But what would it matter to Him? That's the point, isn't it? What does it matter to God?

JAN: I've got this Bible study on fasting that the pastor gave us. Let's look at it.

RON: Let's don't. Let's give it up.

JAN: Ron.

RON: Let's take a look. It can't hurt ... any more than it does.

JAN: C'mon. Look up these references in your Bible.

RON: All right.

JAN: We need some answers.

RON: Look at this. It says here that Jesus fasted forty days.

JAN: Yes, I know. That's why we have forty days of Lent.

RON: And forty nights. But, look, it also says He was hungry. That's an understatement.

JAN: We're in good company, fasting with Jesus.

RON: Oh, look at this. This is the time He was tempted by the devil.

JAN: Sure, in the wilderness.

RON: Jan, I've got it! It's to be strengthened.

JAN: Do you mean we fast and that strengthens us?

RON: It doesn't seem to be true, does it? I feel pretty weak, right now. But, look, if we can be the masters of our own will ...

JAN: You mean with God's help.

RON: Oh, of course, yes. If we are masters of our own will and body, with God's help, then we can be faithful disciples in God's kingdom.

JAN: Of course. That must be it. If we can master our own desires then we can stand against the devil, like Jesus did.

RON: You know what? I still want the dessert.

JAN: So do I, but I think we can make it. I want to.

RON: So do I.

The Night Talker

Theme
"Born Again" — it's a cliché nowadays. But it isn't understood today anymore than when it was first mentioned.

Summary
Nick, the teacher, seeks Jesus, the teacher. He has some questions and Jesus has the answers and the time to explain them. This is a modernization of the Nicodemus-Jesus encounter.

Playing Time	3 minutes
Place	Wherever Jesus spends the night
Props	None
Costumes:	Contemporary, casual
Time	Last night
Cast	JESUS
	NICK — a teacher

NICK: (*ENTERS CAUTIOUSLY*) Teacher?

JESUS: What is it?

NICK: Have you got a minute?

JESUS: It's five hours 'til dawn? I've got lots of time.

NICK: Good. (*PAUSE*) Well, I have a couple of questions.

JESUS: I'd be interested in answering your questions.

NICK: My name is Nick. I've been following your work.

JESUS: My work?

NICK: Your ministry. Your teaching ... God must be with you — all the miracles you've been doing.

JESUS: Are you interested in the kingdom of God?

NICK: Of course. I'm a teacher of God's word, too.

JESUS: I understand that ... but are you interested in the kingdom of God?

NICK: I don't know what you mean.

JESUS: Well, are you interested in the kingdom of God?

NICK: I am interested. Yes, I am.

JESUS: You're sure?

NICK: Yes. Yes. I'm sure.

JESUS: Good. Did you know that you must experience birth again?

NICK: What?

JESUS: Birth — you must experience birth again.

NICK: What are you talking about? How can an adult go through birth again?

JESUS: Nick, now listen to me. You came here to learn right?

NICK: Right.

JESUS: Well, I need you to stick with me on this now.

NICK: What do you mean?

JESUS: Don't get into old habits of intellectualizing what I'm saying. Think, Nick. Think! I need you to think along with me.

NICK: Oh! Oh, all right.

JESUS: Good. Now, for birth into the kingdom of God it takes water and the Spirit.

NICK: Water and the Spirit.

JESUS: When you were born into this world the entire process was a function of the body, right?

NICK: Yes, right.

JESUS: And when you're born into the kingdom it is a work of the Spirit.

NICK: The Spirit?

JESUS: Yes. It's a work of the inner man. And you won't do all the work. The Spirit of God will do a work within you. God will make your spirit new. Like being born for the first time, but it's a spiritual birth not a physical one.

NICK: And the water — that's for repentance of sins.

JESUS: Right.

NICK: The water is outside, cleansing my body, and the Spirit works inside. I'll be a new person on the inside.

JESUS: Right. Listen to the wind. I think it's kicking up a little.

NICK: It'll probably rain. Yesterday, it ...

JESUS: Are you amazed that I said you must be born from above?

NICK: I am a little.

JESUS: Think about that wind. It blows wherever it wants to blow and you don't understand where it comes from or where it is going, do you?

NICK: No, I don't.

JESUS: That's how it is with everyone who is born of the Spirit.

NICK: Now, wait a minute. Let me get this straight. I can be reborn spiritually and I won't understand it but it will happen if I want it to.

JESUS: That's about it.

NICK: I've said it but I really don't understand it.

JESUS: You said you were a teacher of God's word.

NICK: Yes, I am.

JESUS: Then you should be the one to understand.

NICK: Well, I don't. Not fully, I don't.

JESUS: Well, then, just respond to that which you do understand.

NICK: Well, I will think about these things.

JESUS: Remember, don't intellectualize. Just answer God's call.

NICK: Like the wind?

JESUS: Yes, like the wind.

NICK: I'll remember. Good-bye.

JESUS: We'll see each other again.

A Drink Of Water

Theme

No one ever knows when he will be confronted with Jesus. It will change his life.

Summary

A kind gentleman, dressed casually, enters a small restaurant and meets the waitress. He wants a drink of water and she is wondering if it is a good idea to serve him. This is a modernization of the "woman at the well" encounter.

Playing Time	3 minutes
Place	A small restaurant
Props	A towel, a glass of water
Costumes:	Contemporary, casual
Time	Today
Cast	STRANGER — Jesus
	WOMAN — a waitress that the world has abused

WOMAN: *(CLEANING THE COUNTER. THE STRANGER ENTERS AND STANDS, WAITING TO BE SERVED)* What are you doing in here?

STRANGER: I would like a drink.

WOMAN: You're Jewish. I can tell.

STRANGER: And you're very perceptive. Yes, I am a Jew. Now, how about that drink?

WOMAN: You've got your own places. What are you coming in here for?

STRANGER: I was nearby and I was thirsty.

WOMAN: If Max were here he'd throw you out.

STRANGER: Are you going to throw me out?

WOMAN: No, but you'd better leave. Max is due back anytime.

STRANGER: Well, you'd better hurry and give me that drink, then.

WOMAN: Listen ... oh, all right, but don't sit down.

STRANGER: I wouldn't think of it.

WOMAN: (*BRINGING WATER*) There.

STRANGER: (*DRINKING*) Whew. Thanks.

WOMAN: Well?

STRANGER: I said, thanks.

WOMAN: You'd better go.

STRANGER: Max?

WOMAN: Yeah.

STRANGER: What if I told you I could provide you with water that brought life with it?

WOMAN: You're a salesman, right?

STRANGER: I said you were perceptive.

WOMAN: I've known a few salesmen. Do you sell water?

STRANGER: No. I give it away.

WOMAN: No one gives water away.

STRANGER: You just did. I was thirsty. You gave me some water.

WOMAN: (*PAUSE*) Right!

STRANGER: No, really.

WOMAN: (*PAUSE*) Right!

STRANGER: And you could live forever.

WOMAN: Well, I'm game. I could use some of that kind of water. Sounds pretty good to me.

STRANGER: Well?

WOMAN: Well, what? Hey, what are you talking about? Are you going to show me the brochure on the water softener or what?

STRANGER: May I come over to your house tonight and talk to you and your husband about it?

WOMAN: (*PAUSE*) I don't have a husband.

STRANGER: But you've had five, haven't you.

WOMAN: Yes, I've had five, but how ...

STRANGER: And the man you're living with now is not your husband.

WOMAN: Whoa, wait a minute. Oh, I get it; you're religious, aren't you? You know what? People say you have to go to church to be a Christian, but I always thought it was all right just to stay at home and watch the services on TV.

STRANGER: I want to tell you something. Some day church and the TV won't make a bit of difference. What's going to be important is if you know God. To truly know him and worship him. Those are the people that God is looking for.

WOMAN: I know that Jesus will come someday and explain everything to us, all the things we don't understand.

STRANGER: I am the Savior.

WOMAN: You! But you're Jewish.

STRANGER: You are very perceptive.

WOMAN: Oh, I get it. You *are* Jewish. Oh, I must tell everyone. Wait until the night shift gets a load of this. Here is a man who tells me everything I ever did. You have to be Jesus, right? (*THEY SHAKE HANDS*)

A Blind Man Sees

by Jack Bullard and Bob Crowley

Theme

Sometimes the blind can see better than those who have sight.

Summary

A man, blind from birth, is healed by Jesus but faces opposition from the temple authorities. The man sets them straight and then believes in Jesus. A humorous retelling of the old story.

Playing Time	5 minutes
Place	The Holy Land
Props	None
Costumes:	Dog, bird, peasant, Temple official,
Time	Bible times
Cast	DOG — a clever mutt
	DISCIPLE — not as clever as the mutt
	BIRD — a passerby
	JESUS — the leader
	MAN — needs healing
	FATHER
	MOTHER
	NEIGHBOR — lives close by
	OTHER — lives farther away
	PHARISEE — won't live close to anyone
	NARRATOR

NARRATOR: As Jesus was walking one day He saw a man.

DOG: Woof!

NARRATOR: Oh, yes, I forgot, a man with a dog. A seeing-eye dog.

DOG: Woof. That's better.

NARRATOR: I forgot to tell you the man was blind.

DISCIPLE: Teacher, who sinned, this man or his parents, that he should be born blind?

JESUS: Neither this man nor his parents.

DISCIPLE: I don't get it.

JESUS: This happened so that the work of God might be shown in his life. As long as I'm here I must do the work of Him who sent me. While I am in the world I am the light of the world.

NARRATOR: After He said that He spit on the ground.

DOG: Woof. Boy, you have to watch out when people are spitting.

DISCIPLE: It's all right. It's holy spit.

NARRATOR: Are you finished? Good. May I continue? Jesus made some mud with the saliva and put it on the man's eyes and said to him ...

BIRD: (*FLYING BY*) Hey! That's not nice. My mother would never let me play in the mud.

DISCIPLE: That's all right. It's holy mud.

NARRATOR: Well, anyway, Jesus needed some mud. Now that that's settled I will continue. Jesus made the mud and put it on the man's eyes.

116

JESUS: Go wash in the pool of Siloam. (*JESUS EXITS*)

NARRATOR: And he did.

MAN: (*WASHING*) I can see. I really can see.

DOG: Woof. Does this mean I'm fired?

MAN: Why, of course not. I could never get rid of you. You're my friend.

DOG: Woof!

NEIGHBOR: (*ENTERS ALONG WITH OTHER*) Isn't this the man who used to sit and beg?

OTHER: No. He only looks like him.

MAN: I am the man.

DOG: Woof. He is.

NEIGHBOR: How can you see now?

MAN: Do you know Jesus? Well, He put some mud on my eyes and told me to go wash in the pool of Siloam. I did and now I can see.

OTHER: Let's take him to the Pharisees.

NARRATOR: And they did and the Pharisees asked the blind man:

PHARISEE: Did Jesus do this?

MAN: Yes.

PHARISEE: Ah ha, Jesus is working on the Sabbath again.

DOG: Woof. I always worked on the Sabbath. If I hadn't my master would have bumped into things.

PHARISEE: This Jesus cannot be from God because He does not keep the Sabbath.

NEIGHBOR: How can a man who is a sinner perform such signs?

OTHER: I guess there is a division here.

DOG: Woof. I hate division. I rather like addition and subtraction though.

PHARISEE: What do you have to say? It was your eyes He opened.

MAN: He is a prophet.

DOG: Woof. I'll go along with that.

NARRATOR: And the Pharisees still did not believe that the man had been born blind and so they sent for his parents. (*PARENTS ENTER*)

FATHER: (*LOOKING AROUND*) Wow! Nice place.

PHARISEE: Is this your son?

MOTHER AND FATHER: Yep. He's ours.

PHARISEE: Is he the one who was born blind?

MOTHER: Yep. He was born blind.

FATHER: But we don't know how he can see or who opened his eyes.

MOTHER AND FATHER: Ask him. He's old enough to speak for himself.

NARRATOR: And for the second time the Pharisees questioned the man born blind.

MOTHER: Whew!

FATHER: That was close. They could have thrown us out of the synagogue. (*MOTHER AND FATHER EXIT*)

PHARISEE: Give glory to God. We know that this Jesus is a sinner.

MAN: I don't know if He's a sinner or not, but I do know I was blind but now I see.

PHARISEE: What did Jesus do to you? How did He open your eyes?

MAN: I've already told you but you didn't listen. Why do you want to hear it again? Do you want to become His disciples too?

NARRATOR: Then they hurled insults at him.

PHARISEE: You are this Jesus' disciple. We are disciples of Moses. We know God spoke to Moses. As for Jesus, we don't even know where He comes from.

DOG: Woof. Back off, Jack!

MAN: Come here, Fido. Now that is remarkable. You don't know where He comes from yet He opened my eyes. We know God listens to those who do His will. Have you ever heard of a man opening the eyes of a blind man? If this man, Jesus, was not from God He could do nothing.

PHARISEE: You were steeped in sin at birth. How dare you lecture us! (*MAN IS THROWN OUT*)

DOG: Woof, WOOF! (*DOG CHASES PHARISEE OUT AND THEN RETURNS TO MASTER*)

JESUS: (*ENTERS*) I knew they had thrown you out of the synagogue so I've been looking for you. Do you believe in the Son of Man?

MAN: Who is He, Sir? Tell me so that I may believe in Him.

JESUS: You have now seen Him. In fact, He is the one speaking to you.

MAN: (*KNEELING*) Lord, I believe. (*PHARISEE ENTERS*)

JESUS: I came into the world to judge so that the blind will see and those who see will become blind.

PHARISEE: What, are we blind too?

JESUS: If you were blind you would not be guilty of sin, but since you say you see, your guilt remains.

DOG: Woof! And you call me a dog.

Talk Show II

Theme

Everyone has to obey the voice of Jesus sooner or later, so you might as well do it while you can rejoice about it.

Summary

This is a TV talk show featuring Mary, Martha and Lazarus and a lively discussion about Lazarus' death and Jesus bringing him back to life.

Playing Time	3 minutes
Place	A TV studio
Props	None
Costumes:	Contemporary, appropriate for a talk show
Time	Today
Cast	PHIL DENNEHY — talk show host
	LAZARUS — the person Jesus raised from the dead
	MARY — his sister
	MARTHA — his other sister

PHIL: (*WALKING AROUND USING A HAND-HELD MICRO-PHONE TALKING TO FOUR PANELISTS SEATED IN CHAIRS*) You've met these ladies before. Meet Mary and her sister Martha and you'll remember their brother Lazarus. Now this family has a unique story to relate. You see, Lazarus has been raised from the dead by Jesus.

LAZARUS: That's right. I was dead. I was really dead.

MARY: He's the baby of the family. We are so happy that Jesus is our Messiah and our friend. Jesus came and raised Lazarus from the dead.

MARTHA: I was a little miffed at Jesus.

MARY: Martha, this isn't the place for that. We should be joyful that our brother has been restored to us.

MARTHA: I couldn't be more joyful. I just express it differently, that's all.

MARY: I guess you do.

LAZARUS: Please, Mary, don't start on that again.

MARTHA: Miffed. Maybe I was more than a little miffed. Let's face it, I was angry with Jesus. Hadn't we seen Jesus heal the blind people? Hadn't He healed others from leprosy? Jesus could have certainly healed Lazarus if He had been there when he got sick.

MARY: Actually, He had raised people from the dead before Lazarus.

LAZARUS: That's right. We heard the stories.

PHIL: Now, wait a minute. Are you telling me that Jesus had raised others from the dead before Lazarus?

LAZARUS: Exactly. On two occasions.

MARTHA: We only heard about it, though. It is a bit different when you experience death yourself.

LAZARUS: I'll say.

PHIL: So, if you knew about Jesus raising others from the dead, why couldn't you have the faith that Jesus would raise Lazarus from the dead?

MARTHA: You have to understand, we had faith but not that much faith. We trusted Jesus and knew that we would see Lazarus again in the last day, but I for one just didn't have faith that Jesus would raise him right then.

PHIL: And how about you, Mary, how did you feel?

MARY: Well, to tell you the truth, I didn't have the faith either. I was pretty caught up in my grief. If you've never gone through the death of someone near to you, you don't know what I mean. I was really grieving and nothing could break through that. Not even the comforting words of my friends.

PHIL: And what did Jesus do?

MARTHA: Well, we could see that He was moved.

MARY: Moved is too gentle a word. He was, well, it looked like He was angry.

PHIL: Angry? Jesus was angry?

MARTHA: It looked that way to me.

PHIL: Why should He be angry? At you for lack of faith?

MARTHA: No, no, I don't think so.

MARY: We talked about this a lot. I think it was because He was encountering death. I think He was angry at the hold it has on us. It is so powerful and we often think about it a lot. Death was, at that time, the stronghold of Satan.

PHIL: I see. So, Jesus was probably angry at death and Satan.

LAZARUS: I agree. If you're going to be angry that's a good target.

MARTHA: The rest was just God, the Father, working through Jesus. Jesus simply called to Lazarus.

PHIL: And he came out of the grave.

LAZARUS: It was just that simple. I obeyed.

MARY: And we rejoiced.

LAZARUS: Everyone had to obey the voice of Jesus sooner or later.

MARY: So you might as well do it while you can rejoice about it.

PHIL: All right, that's our show for this week, but wait, we haven't heard from Pastor Ames, yet. (*USE YOUR PASTOR'S NAME*) Pastor, what do you think?

Life

Theme

If we trust Jesus He is with us empowering us with the Holy Spirit just like the disciples when Jesus breathed on them.

Summary

Peter, confronted with the death of a girl, relies on what Jesus taught him. A reader's theatre presentation.

Playing Time	9 minutes
Place	A neutral reading area
Props	Four stools, wine skin, four glasses, bread
Costumes:	Contemporary, casual
Time	Storytelling time
Cast	FIRST READER — female, soprano
	SECOND READER — male, bass
	THIRD READER — female, alto
	FOURTH READER — male, tenor

(READERS ENTER AND SIT ON STOOLS. WINE, GLASSES, AND BREAD ARE ON TABLE)

SECOND: *Shema, Israel, Adonai elohenu, Adonai ehad.*

FOURTH: Hear, oh Israel, the Lord our God, the Lord is one.

SECOND: *(POURING WINE AND RAISING A GLASS)* Blessed are you, O Lord, King of the universe who created the fruit of the vine. We thank you, our Father, for the holy vine of your servant

David which you have made known to us through Jesus, the Messiah. To you be glory forever. (*THEY ALL DRINK. SECOND READER HOLDS THE BREAD ALOFT*)

Blessed are you. O Lord our God, King of the whole world, you who bring forth bread out of the earth. (*HE BREAKS THE BREAD*) We thank you, our Father, for the life and the knowledge which you have made known to us through your servant Jesus. To you be glory forever. (*THEY EAT AND DRINK*)

FIRST: The holy man of God began to eat. He was tired and hungry after the day's work. Not that he wasn't used to work. Not too many years ago he had spent many long hard nights weathered by the spray of the waves on the sea of Galilee.

THIRD: Now he sought another type of fish, the elusive soul of man. It still was not an easy life. Souls were just as difficult as fish to catch, but he liked the challenge and lately the nets were bulging with the harvest.

SECOND: It's peaceful here. Everything is so green this time of year.

FOURTH: Our rainy season is quite long here and the sea keeps the temperature low, so it's good for crops.

FIRST: And Lydda is just far enough off the Jerusalem-Joppa road so that not too many travelers pass this way.

THIRD: We're honored that you've come to be with us for a while, Peter.

SECOND: There are people everywhere who are now trusting the Messiah. I hope to visit as many as possible.

FOURTH: You'll have many more to visit after what happened yesterday and today.

FIRST: Yes. The story of how you healed Aeneas is being told everywhere.

SECOND: Yes, it's a good thing, but you must remember it wasn't I who did it, it was God. God healed Aeneas. Only He could do that.

FOURTH: Yes, the Lord God healed me. Praise His name. But what I don't understand us is how it happened. It's so wonderful! Paralyzed for eight years, and in an instant I'm up and moving around, as if I'd never been sick. How can this happen?

SECOND: My whole life with the Messiah has been a learning process. I was the last to learn most of the truths He taught, but He kept telling me in different ways until I finally understood. He's not physically with me now but nothing has changed. By the power of the Holy Spirit He's still teaching me.

FOURTH: It does seem strange. I don't know, all of a sudden I didn't think like a paralyzed man anymore. You said "Jesus the Messiah makes you whole," and I just got up.

FIRST: Loud knocking interrupted the meal and when the door was opened two travelers burst into the room almost knocking Aeneas down.

FOURTH: Peter! Peter! Come with us. We need you.

SECOND: Calm yourselves. Sit and rest and tell me of the desperate need.

FOURTH: We're from Joppa. There's a group of people there who believe that Jesus of Nazareth is the Messiah. Well, one of the widows of the group, Tabitha is her name, just died. She had been sick for about a week. The leaders sent us to ask you to come immediately. Come with us, Peter.

SECOND: How far is Joppa?

FOURTH: About half a day's journey. But we just made it in half that time. We have a donkey; that will help, but we must go, it's getting dark.

SECOND: Finish your wine. I had intended to visit our brothers and sisters in Joppa anyway.

THIRD: The men finished their wine and bread and bid farewell to the house of Aeneas and were on their way, taking turns riding on the donkey.

FIRST: The cool night air, the close companionship, and the urgency of their mission sped them on their way and soon the thriving port of Joppa could be seen as they swiftly descended the last hill. (*FIRST AND THIRD READERS BEGIN TO WAIL*)

FOURTH: This is the house of Tabitha.

SECOND: Where is she?

FOURTH: Thank you for coming, Peter. She's upstairs. The women have prepared the body for your blessing.

FIRST: The fisherman slowly ascended the stairs and entered the room and saw the dead body of Tabitha.

THIRD: Look. Look at the fine work our dear dead sister has done.

FIRST: Fine linen garments stitched by her loving hands.

FOURTH: She was a good woman, loving and kind and well loved by our community.

SECOND: Yes, I can see that. She was well loved. Now, leave me alone with her. I'll be downstairs later.

FIRST: He knelt by the body and gazed into the darkness of the clear, cool night.

SECOND: (*PRAYING*) Lord God, King of the universe, You who set the stars in their place, and breathed life into man, I honor You. I glorify You. You gave us the perfect life of Your son, Jesus.

Hail to You, Jesus, Messiah, Son of the Most High God. Blessed be Your holy name. It was Your promise and Your will that provided our Comforter, the Holy Spirit.

Praise be to You, Holy Spirit of God. It was Your power that Elijah called upon to raise the widow's son. Elisha also raised a dead son by Your power. You gave power to the Master to raise the son of the widow of Nain. And the daughter of Jairus. And Lazarus. A word from You would awake the sleeping Tabitha. Oh, Lord God, send back the spirit into her body. Tabitha arise!

FIRST: Peter could see her breathing again and he silently thanked his Master.

FOURTH: Her eyes opened wide. She looked around the room and saw Peter.

FIRST: She sat up.

THIRD: Peter helped her to stand and after they embraced Peter called the others into the room.

FOURTH: The mournful sound of wailing was exchanged for the joyful sound of celebration. (*ALL SING A JOYFUL PRAISE SONG*)

Walk With Him

Theme

Jesus is with us even though we can't see Him.

Summary

Two disciples of Jesus, Cleopas and his companion, have just encountered Jesus and talk about what it meant to them.

Playing Time	4 minutes
Setting	On the road from Jerusalem to Emmaus
Props	None
Costumes	Disciple of Jesus
Time	Easter afternoon
Cast	CLEOPAS — a follower of Jesus
	COMPANION — also a follower of Jesus

CLEOPAS: (*RUNNING IN*) Where'd he go!

COMPANION: (*FOLLOWING*) How should I know? Jesus was with us and then He just vanished.

CLEOPAS: Jesus is alive!

COMPANION: I know. I know. But where is He now?

CLEOPAS: We've got to tell the others.

COMPANION: Are you crazy? We just came from Jerusalem. That's a long walk — seven miles — and you want to go back?

CLEOPAS: How do you feel?

COMPANION: Great.

CLEOPAS: I haven't felt like this in a long time. I feel great too.

COMPANION: My heart is like it's on fire and it won't stop burning.

CLEOPAS: Mine too. I felt that way when He used to teach us. Here we are just walking along and all of a sudden there He was, walking with us. You didn't recognize Him, did you?

COMPANION: No, I didn't and you didn't either.

CLEOPAS: You know I didn't. I was depressed about the cruci-fixion. All our lives had been changed by Him and then suddenly He was dead.

COMPANION: Anyway, we didn't recognize Him. And then you said, "Are you the only one ..."

CLEOPAS: No, don't you remember? He asked us what we were talking about. And then I answered His question with a question. I asked Him if He was the only visitor to Jerusalem who didn't know what was happening.

COMPANION: And then He asked what we meant. I told Him, about Jesus of Nazareth, and how He was a prophet who performed mighty miracles and was a great preacher, blessed by God and how all the people loved Him.

CLEOPAS: Then I told Him about how the chief priests and rul-ers sentenced Jesus to death and crucified Him. And do you re-member what I said next?

COMPANION: You said something about Jesus being the Messiah.

CLEOPAS: Right. I told Him we had our hopes pinned on Jesus to deliver Israel.

COMPANION: Then I said that now it is the third day since His death. I told Him what the women said who had been to the tomb this morning — how it was empty and they saw the vision of angels who told them Jesus had risen from the dead.

CLEOPAS: I thought what they said was nonsense.

COMPANION: We all thought it was nonsense.

CLEOPAS: I do remember Jesus telling us that, now.

COMPANION: I remember that. But I sure didn't believe those women.

CLEOPAS: He called us fools for not believing. That hurt.

COMPANION: It hurts when I'm slow to believe. It hurts even more when Jesus recognizes it.

CLEOPAS: But at the same time He was patient with us. He did explain all the prophecies in the scriptures to us that referred to Him.

COMPANION: That was great. I liked that. And then when He arrived here He acted like He was leaving.

CLEOPAS: You know that was strange, His acting like He was going to travel on.

COMPANION: I've been thinking about that. I guess He just wanted to make sure we wanted to hear about Jesus.

CLEOPAS: I didn't know who He was, but my heart was on fire because of His teaching and I wanted to hear more.

COMPANION: We should have known it was Jesus. No one has ever taught like that.

CLEOPAS: We just couldn't see.

COMPANION: And then He took bread and blessed it and broke it and kept giving it to us to eat.

CLEOPAS: That's when I recognized Him. Then I knew it was Jesus.

COMPANION: I recognized Him when He broke the bread, too. And then He vanished.

CLEOPAS: Do you know what? He's still here.

COMPANION: What?

CLEOPAS: He's still here. We just can't see Him anymore. He's still here. He's with us. He *is* alive. We have to go back to Jerusalem and tell the others.

COMPANION: Seven miles — why not. Then you can explain what you mean. (*THEY BEGIN TO WALK SLOWLY OFF*)

CLEOPAS: Well, He is God. He must be or He wouldn't be alive after He was dead, right?

COMPANION: Right.

CLEOPAS: And God has no limits, right?

COMPANION: Right.

CLEOPAS: Well, that's what He was trying to teach us. He was walking and we didn't know who He was, then we recognized Him and then we couldn't see Him. Don't you get it? Just because we can't see Him doesn't mean He isn't here. He will always be with us. He's alive!

The Church

Theme

The church has had turmoil from the start. It was as difficult then as it is now. The church can only survive if Jesus is the head.

Summary

A mysterious visitor from church "headquarters" calls on the Rev. John Baxter, pastor of a modern day church that is having some major problems. The visitor proposes some startling answers for the church's dilemma and firmly implants the solution by a unique object lesson from history.

Playing Time	10 minutes
Place	A church meeting room and then thirty years after the time of Christ
Props	Coffee cups and coffee pot
Costumes	Contemporary and Bible character costumes
Time	The present and Bible times
Cast	JIM — a businessman
	MARTHA — a homemaker
	PETE — a businessman
	JOHN — their pastor
	GUY — a visitor

JIM: (*ENTERS WITH MARTHA. JIM POURS TWO CUPS OF COFFEE*) Where is Pete? I want to get this over with and get home. I brought a briefcase full of papers home and I haven't touched them yet.

MARTHA: He said we'd start at seven tonight.

PETE: (*ENTERS AND POURS HIMSELF A CUP OF COFFEE*) Well, well, I guess no one's late if they're here before the boss.

JIM: I was even here on time for a change. Now it's your turn.

PETE: I was actually here on time but I stopped in to talk to Pastor John and well, we got to talking — I invited him to our meeting.

JIM: Do you think we need help?

PETE: Frankly, yes, I think we do. The board meets Tuesday, you know, and I've got to present some sound suggestions to them. I invited John only because of the gentleman I met in his office. He's from headquarters. They'll drop in later.

JIM: I think we've accomplished quite a lot.

MARTHA: We sure did.

PETE: When the board reviews our progress they won't see any.

JIM: Pete, I think we can be satisfied with the suggestions we've made.

MARTHA: Jim is right. Let's review the ideas we have and decide which one to present to the board. (*LOOKING AT HER NOTES*) Number one was to advertise in the paper.

PETE: I don't like making a business out of Christianity.

MARTHA: Next was a radio broadcast.

JIM: Don't we have enough "holy Joes" on the radio already?

PETE: We all agreed that taping the morning worship would not relate to the community what this church is trying to say.

JIM: Who said we want to relate to the community? This committee was formed to find ways to get more money from the congregation. We've got our church to worry about.

PETE: Jim, if we don't start showing that we care about the people in the community, we won't have a church. Our church members come from the community.

JIM: The church will be okay. It's existed for two thousand years.

MARTHA: Yes, by being a vital force in the community.

JIM: The church has to look out for its own. We can't be giving our money and precious time and just letting anyone use our building. If you open yourself up to the community every wretched person within fifty miles will be streaming in here with their hand out. This is a sophisticated congregation and we just can't have anyone and everyone walking in here any time they want to. We have to protect ourselves.

PETE: I think you're getting way off the subject, Jim.

JIM: Well, I just don't like the idea of always looking for ways to spend the church's money. I volunteered for this committee because I felt the church needs more money. The way inflation is hitting everyone's pocketbook ... (*JOHN AND GUY ENTER AND SIT A LITTLE APART FROM THE OTHERS*)

PETE: John, come on up here where you can hear. (*JOHN BEGINS TO RISE BUT GUY RESTRAINS HIM WITH A HAND*)

JOHN: No, this will do fine. Let me introduce Guy.

GUY: Not necessary, really. Just call me Guy.

PETE: And this is Martha and Jim.

GUY: Glad to meet you.

PETE: Let me brief you on what we've covered so far.

GUY: No need. I heard everything. Please continue. Just pretend I'm not here.

PETE: Maybe you've had some experience with this problem before, Guy?

GUY: Let's just say it's nothing new.

PETE: Well, If you have anything to say, feel free to enter right in. We were just reviewing some of our ideas. Martha, will you continue?

MARTHA: Jim's idea was next. He wanted to increase our efforts with the annual pledges of money.

JIM: I think if it's presented right the people will accept it. And I don't mean a hard-sell campaign. You can tell people about needs without forcing them to help.

What I meant was providing the canvassers with a few courses on how to present the needs of the church to the members. I thought it would also help if we provided some attractive loose-leaf notebooks with colored photos of some of the activities of the church. The need for next year could be easily explained by the canvasser and easily understood by the members of the congregation.

PETE: What about the cost?

JIM: I think the really important part of my suggestion is not the cost but the personal contact that the church member has through the canvasser.

JOHN: I know Jim has been interested in this sort of extended campaign for some time.

JIM: I sure have. Ever since last year when I was the chairman of the campaign. I know how many thousands we were short and I just think it'll be worse this year if we don't take some action now.

PETE: Does anyone have any questions for Jim? No? Martha.

MARTHA: There's only one suggestion left and that's mine. I'll tell you briefly what it is. My idea was to begin an evangelism program. It really changes the lives of everyone connected with it.

JOHN: I've read about some of those programs, but I'd like to hear more about your idea, Martha.

MARTHA: The interesting thing about the program is the changed lives of the people who participate. In the process of telling other people about God's plan of salvation for their lives the participants are soon seeking a deeper commitment to Christ themselves.

JOHN: The churches that have this program — has there been any increase in their membership?

MARTHA: Yes, but the dramatic increase is in the church income. That's it, Pete.

PETE: Thanks, Martha. I guess I'm the only one who hasn't had a brainstorm of some kind for this committee. But I did come up with something and that is to hire a professional fund-raiser.

JIM: Are you kidding? Do you realize how much those guys charge? They don't charge a flat rate, you know. They want a percentage and it isn't a small percentage either.

PETE: Wait a minute. I was thinking it would be a good idea to set a minimum amount for the guy to raise and pay him a certain percentage only if he reached that minimum. The trick would be to set the minimum higher than last year's total.

JIM: I don't think our congregation will like some outsider running the entire campaign. At least with my idea the canvasser will be a fellow member, not some stranger working for a fee.

PETE: He won't do the calling himself. He just trains our own people to be more effective when they make their visits.

JIM: You don't think he'll call on the more wealthy members himself? He certainly will. He'll go right along with John, here, and convince them to donate more money. Of course he will. It's money in his pocket.

MARTHA: This is all well and good, but I think the emphasis should be on spreading the gospel.

JIM: I still think we ought to concentrate on the members we already have — encourage them to give more. This is just between us but I happen to know a lot of people that are better off than I am and give a lot less. We got into a discussion in our Sunday school class and a lot of people admitted giving less each week to the church than they spent on dining out. The Bible says: "It is more blessed to give than to receive."

MARTHA: Well, If you're going to start quoting the Bible to reinforce your arguments I think you ought to include the verse that commands us to go and tell all nations ...

PETE: I suppose I could present all the suggestions to the board.

JIM: I don't think all of them are worthy of presentation.

JOHN: I've kept out of this discussion so far, but I think it may be time for me to intervene. First of all, I think each one of you has some very good suggestions. Now, I know I'm not on this committee, but Pete asked us to help with some suggestions of our own, so since I missed the beginning of the meeting, let me ask one thing: Did you start this meeting with a prayer?

PETE: No, we didn't. We never start any of our business meetings with a prayer.

JIM: Nor do we start our prayer meetings with church business.

JOHN: Let me suggest a prayer now. I think we could use some help from God. (*PRAYING*) Dear Father, we are in need of some answers to our problem of a dwindling congregation and maybe what's worse, dwindling income. It's not for ourselves we ask, Lord, it's for all the cutbacks we've had to make in our help to the missionaries. Dear Lord, just give us the answers we need, in the name of our dear Savior, Amen.

JIM: I just hope we can come to a conclusion soon.

PETE: John, what other suggestions do you have for us?

JOHN: Actually I was going to suggest reading a Bible verse.

JIM: Oh, for crying out loud, I have lots of work to do at home. Can't we get on with it? Let's just vote on the suggestions we have.

PETE: A vote? How can we vote? There's only three of us. We'd never get a majority on any suggestion.

JIM: Well, the prayer sure didn't help.

GUY: (*RAISING HIS HAND. JIM, PETE AND MARTHA FREEZE*) I think we could use a little lesson here.

JOHN: A lesson? What is this? What have you done?

GUY: (*WRAPPING CLOAKS AROUND THE COMMITTEE MEMBERS AND DRAPING THEIR HEADS WITH COVERINGS. THEY ARE BECOMING NEW TESTAMENT CHARACTERS*) I'm just arranging things so they can relate to an important time in church history.

JAMES: So, what will we do?

MARTHA: I don't know.

PETER: The elders are expecting an answer.

JOHN: What is going on? I don't understand.

GUY: You will, if you want to.

JOHN: They're not acting, are they?

GUY: No, they're not acting.

JOHN: Then, what?

GUY: Just living — in another time.

JOHN: The past.

GUY: Yes. The past to you. The present to them.

MARTHA: My suggestion will require no expenditure and, I'm sure, prove to be quite rewarding.

JAMES: Martha, we appreciate your presence here, but I think the problem is one which can best be solved through the application of economic principles. Since no one expects you to be experienced in these things, I think this rather involved matter should be handled by those who are experienced.

MARTHA: But, I thought ...

PETER: Now, just a minute, James. I invited Martha here to help us. As a representative of the unattached women in the church she has a right to be heard and I'll have to ask you to be respectful.

MARTHA: I don't think we should be arguing. We've got a problem to solve. I don't think it can ever be solved unless we help each other.

JAMES: We've got to be sensible.

JOHN: (*RUNNING INTO THE MIDST OF THE COMMITTEE*) Stop! This is getting nowhere! (*TO GUY*) This isn't working. You've set them in this different time but they haven't learned anything. (*THE COMMITTEE FREEZES*)

GUY: Well, maybe you can teach them.

JOHN: Me?

GUY: You are their leader. Here. (*HANDING JOHN A COSTUME*)

JOHN: What can I do?

GUY: Lead. (*HELPING HIM INTO COSTUME*)

JOHN: They've stopped.

GUY: I stopped them. As you said, they were getting nowhere.

JOHN: How can this be happening?

GUY: Let's just say that God is the beginning and the end.

JOHN: Tell me something. This is the early church, isn't it? Well, then how can these people have lived so near the time that Jesus was on the earth and not trust Him?

GUY: Thirty years.

JOHN: Thirty years since Jesus left them? Thirty years. They've strayed so far in thirty years? What's wrong with these people? (*WALKING AMONG THE FROZEN COMMITTEE. POINTING TO PETER*) I'm inclined to agree with him. But she has a good idea, too. But she's a woman. They'll never listen to her. And what about you? (*INDICATING JAMES*) What's your answer? I know, making sure the people will give their tithe. Asking them to make a pledge. (*INDICATING PETER*) But then he says that will give the church too much power over the individual. (*GUY LIFTS HIS HAND AND THE COMMITTEE UNFREEZES*)

JAMES: Ah, here's John Mark. Here's some help for us.

MARTHA: You've got to help us. Didn't He say, go into all the world? Tell us what Jesus said.

JOHN: Let me read it to you from my writing. Yes, Jesus said, "Go into all the world and preach the good news to all creation." Let me tell you a story.

You've all heard the story of Pentecost when we all received the power of the Holy Spirit. Well, shortly after that we began meeting together. The Holy Spirit was drawing us together.

We met every day at the Temple to worship God and to minister to each other and to witness our faith to the unbelievers. There were quite a lot of people meeting each day. Those were great days. We loved being together so we would continue the meetings in someone's house after sundown. Many times it was my cousin Barnabas' house where I also lived.

Those were thrilling times. We would eat together, sing the praises of God, pray and listen to the stories, usually told by Simon Peter or John, the brother of James. Stories about their life with Jesus. We never tired of hearing the same stories over and over.

We shared our love and our possessions. But here is the real miracle. And it's one we took for granted for quite a while: People were beginning to join us. Our number increased tremendously. People were drawn to our group, so much so that we had to begin meeting in several different locations. We didn't actually seek

143

new believers. The Lord provided the increase. He did it; not us. It was a blessing to see the Lord work.

So, that's my story. Simple, isn't it. But it's true. All that is necessary is that you do what is expected of you and the Lord will provide the increase.

You should pray together, minister to each other's needs, and study the words of Jesus. (*JOHN AND GUY EXIT*)

JAMES: There's got to be more to it than that.

MARTHA: I believe him. I think he wanted to help us. We must listen to him.

JAMES: All that singing and praying — I can see why they didn't get anything accomplished — wasting half the night.

PETER: I trust him, but thirty years is a long time. His ways were right for that time, but today is today.

JAMES: We have to get things done today. It's a modern world.

In My Father's House

Theme

The vain philosophies of this world don't prepare us to handle the really difficult problems of life.

Summary

Jeremy visits his dying mother. She knows she is dying and she asks her son for some help in understanding a Bible passage that could help her die peacefully. Jeremy cannot help.

Playing Time	3 minutes
Place	A nursing home
Props	Wheelchair, balloons, card, note pad
Costumes	Jeremy — Contemporary
	Mom — Robe, gown, slippers
Time	The present
Cast	JEREMY
	MOM

MOM: (*ENTERS IN WHEELCHAIR*) Jeremy, you came.

JEREMY: (*ENTERS WITH BALLOONS AND A CARD*) I wanted to. (*AN AWKWARD SILENCE*) How do you feel?

MOM: Tired. I'm so tired. (*SHE CRIES*) I have no strength. I'm just so tired.

JEREMY: Uh, Mom. You'll get better soon. I know you will.

MOM: No, Jeremy. Not this time. Not this time.

JEREMY: Uh, Mom, you and Dad always take that vacation to Florida. Don't you want to go to Florida?

MOM: No, I don't. I don't want to go to Florida. I'm too tired.

JEREMY: Mom, you'll be all right.

MOM: No, Jeremy, I won't.

JEREMY: But Mom, there's lots to live for. You've got to be positive. Have hope. Think positive thoughts.

MOM: About what?

JEREMY: About getting well. You're the one who always told me to be positive about everything.

MOM: And were you?

JEREMY: Usually. It's a good way to live. It worked for me. It worked for you.

MOM: It used to work for me.

JEREMY: What happened?

MOM: Being positive is great when things are going well. And even sometimes when things don't go well. Now I've come up against something too big to be positive about.

JEREMY: Then I'll help. I can think positive thoughts along with you.

MOM: Jeremy, you're not facing death right now. I am — alone.

JEREMY: It doesn't seem fair.

MOM: No, son, it isn't fair. I've had a lot of time to think since I've been sick and I listen to the radio a lot. Some preacher was on the other day and he read from the Bible. Here, I wrote it down. (*SEARCHING FOR A NOTE PAD*) Here it is.

"Do not let your hearts be troubled. Trust in God, trust also in me. In my father's house are many rooms; if it were not so, I would have told you. I am going there to prepare a place for you, I will come back and take you to be with me that you also may be where I am. You know the way to the place where I am going."

JEREMY: That's very comforting.

MOM: No, it's not. What's it mean?

JEREMY: I don't know. How should I know?

MOM: It's not comforting. Not a bit. I don't know what it means. I'm dying and I'm tired and I don't know what it means. (*SHE CRIES*)

JEREMY: Hey, Mom, don't worry your pretty little head about it. Think positive. Don't concern yourself with something no one can understand. Look, I brought you a card and look at these balloons. That should cheer you up. (*MOM LEAVES CRYING. JEREMY FOLLOWS*)

147

Creation

Theme
The majesty of God's creation.

Summary
The creation story. Reader's theatre.

Playing Time	5 minutes
Place	A neutral reading area
Props	Black folders with scripts
Costumes	Black
Time	The time before time
Cast	FIRST READER
	SECOND READER

FIRST: (*ENTERS ALONG WITH SECOND READER*) In the beginning **God** ... (*READ SIMULTANEOUSLY WITH SECOND READER*)

SECOND: ... **God** created the heavens and the earth.

BOTH: Now the earth was a formless void.

SECOND: And God's Spirit moved upon the face of the waters.

BOTH: God said,

FIRST: Let there be light.

BOTH: And there was light.

SECOND: God saw the light, that it was good and God divided the light from the darkness.

BOTH: God called the light ...

FIRST: Day.

BOTH: And the darkness He called ...

FIRST: Night.

SECOND: Evening came and morning came.

BOTH: The first day. *(PAUSE)* God said,

FIRST: Let there be a firmament in the midst of the waters dividing the vapor above from the water below.

BOTH: And it was so. And God called the firmament ...

FIRST: Heaven.

SECOND: Evening came and morning came.

BOTH: The second day. *(PAUSE)* God said,

FIRST: Let the waters under the heavens be gathered together into one place and let the dry land appear.

BOTH: And it was so. God called the dry land ...

FIRST: Earth.

BOTH: And the waters that were gathered together He called,

FIRST: Seas.

BOTH: And God saw that it was good. And God said,

FIRST: Let the earth put forth vegetation.

BOTH: And it was so. And God saw that it was good.

SECOND: Evening came and morning came.

BOTH: The third day. (*PAUSE*) God said,

FIRST: Let there be lights in the firmament of the heaven to separate the day from the night.

BOTH: And it was so.

SECOND: God made the two great lights, the greater light to rule the day and the lesser light to rule the night. He made the stars also.

BOTH: God set them in the sky to light the earth. And God saw that it was good.

SECOND: Evening came and morning came.

BOTH: The fourth day. (*PAUSE*) God said,

FIRST: Let the waters bring forth abundantly living creatures and let birds fly in the heavens above the earth.

SECOND: So God created every kind of sea creature and every kind of bird.

BOTH: And God saw that it was good. God blessed them saying,

FIRST: Be fruitful and multiply and fill the waters and the earth.

SECOND: Evening came and morning came.

BOTH: The fifth day. *(PAUSE)* God said,

FIRST: Let the earth bring forth living creatures according to their kinds, cattle and creeping things and beasts of the earth.

SECOND: God made all sorts of wild animals and cattle and creeping things.

BOTH: And God saw that it was good. Then God said,

FIRST: Let us make man in Our image, after Our own likeness to have dominion over all things and over all the earth.

SECOND: So God created man in His own image, in the image of God He created him, male and female He created them.

BOTH: God blessed them and God said to them,

FIRST: Be fruitful and multiply and fill the earth and subdue it. And have dominion over the fish of the sea and the birds of the air and over every living thing that moves upon the earth.

BOTH: God blessed them.

SECOND: God saw all that He had made,

BOTH: And it was good.

SECOND: Evening came and morning came.

BOTH: The sixth day.

SECOND: Thus the heavens and the earth were completed and all that they contained.

BOTH: And on the seventh day God finished His work.

SECOND: He rested the seventh day from all His work which He had done.

BOTH: So God blessed the seventh day and declared it holy,

SECOND: Because on the seventh day **God rested** ... (*READ SIMULTANEOUSLY*)

BOTH: ... **God rested** from all the work He had done in creation.

Everyman And Woman

Theme

The church as the body of Christ is "in the world" and needs to relate to spiritual things but keep its feet firmly planted on solid ground. How does it do that? Confession leads to forgiveness.

Summary

A rehearsal for the medieval play *Everyman* erupts into an argument when the actor playing Everyman cannot confess.

Playing Time	7 minutes
Place	Your church
Props	None
Costumes	Medieval
Time	The present
Cast	EVERYMAN
	CONSCIENCE — a woman
	CONFESSION — a woman

(*A REHEARSAL FOR EVERYMAN*)

EVERYMAN: Oh, you give me great contentment, Conscience, certainly, with your sweet words.

CONSCIENCE: Now, let us go together, Everyman, lovingly to that cleansing river, Confession.

EVERYMAN: Oh, I weep for joy; I wish we were there! but, I beg you to tell me, if you will, where Confession, that holy man, dwells.

CONSCIENCE: In the house of salvation; we shall find him in that place, that shall comfort us, by God's grace. (*CONSCIENCE TAKES EVERYMAN TO CONFESSION*) Here is Confession. Kneel down and ask mercy. For he is highly esteemed by God Almighty.

EVERYMAN: Oh, glorious fountain, that purifies all uncleanliness, wash the dark spots of vice from me. I come with Conscience for my redemption, and offer sincere and complete repentance; for I am commanded a pilgrimage to take, and a strict account before God to make. Oh, hear me, Confession, guide to salvation. (*PAUSE*) Oh hear me, Confession, guide to salvation. (*SOMETHING IS WRONG. EVERYMAN WHISPERS TO CONFESSION*) I well know your sorrow. (*NO RESPONSE*) I well know your sorrow.

CONFESSION: I know my line. I didn't drop a line. You did. (*TO CONSCIENCE*) What's the line?

CONSCIENCE: Everyman, it's your line. You're supposed to say, "Help my good deeds; oh answer my plea!"

EVERYMAN: That's not my line.

CONSCIENCE: Of course it's your line. You're supposed to say, "Help my good deeds; oh answer my plea!" It rhymes with her line, "And because with Conscience you come to me."

EVERYMAN: It's not my line.

CONSCIENCE: It is your line. Here's the script.

EVERYMAN: It's not my line.

CONSCIENCE: You always go up on that line. Here it is. Right here. "Oh, glorious fountain, that purifies all uncleanliness, wash blah, blah, blah, vice from me. I come with Conscience for my redemption, and blah, blah, blah, complete repentance; for I am

154

blah, blah, blah to take, and a strict account before God to make."
Listen to this, "Oh, hear me, confession, guide to salvation. Help
my good Deeds; oh, answer my plea."

EVERYMAN: Let me see that. (*GRABBING THE BOOK AWAY
FROM CONFESSION, EVERYMAN SEES THAT HE IS WRONG
AND MAKES AN EXCUSE FOR FORGETTING HIS LINE*) I've
had to work overtime four times this week.

CONSCIENCE: Can we get back to it? Listen, Everyman, why
don't you just admit you messed up the line and we can continue
the rehearsal.

EVERYMAN: Do you know how much sleep I got last night?

CONSCIENCE: Of course I know how much sleep you got. You
got five hours sleep.

EVERYMAN: Yeah. That's right. Five hours. How did you
know?

CONSCIENCE: You told us when you forgot your blocking.
You always make some excuse when you make a mistake.

EVERYMAN: Well, okay, I made a mistake. Big deal. I have a
lot of pressure. My stupid boss messes up too. He messed up an
entire run and I had to work overtime to fix it.

CONFESSION: Let's go back a bit to where you kneel to Confession and say ...

EVERYMAN: Boy, oh boy. You're getting a kick out of this,
aren't you?

CONFESSION: Getting a kick out of what?

CONSCIENCE: You're going to get a kick out of me leaving.

EVERYMAN: Out of me kneeling to you.

CONFESSION: It's in the script.

EVERYMAN: I know that, but you enjoy a man kneeling in front of you, don't you?

CONFESSION: Get off it. It's in the script. I'm Confession, you're Everyman. Let's get on with it.

CONSCIENCE: Please.

EVERYMAN: Okay, but I'm going to at least play it standing up. People pray standing up.

CONSCIENCE: It's true they do. I am right now. (*GIVING EVERYMAN HIS LINE*) Oh, glorious fountain ...

EVERYMAN: There, you see. She smiled. Did you see her smile? She's enjoying this.

CONFESSION: I always smile when I first see you.

EVERYMAN: You do? Why?

CONFESSION: It's part of my motivation. I'm glad to see a sinner approach the Almighty by confessing his sins.

EVERYMAN: The script says, "I beg you to tell me, if you will, where Confession, that holy *man* dwells." Why do you have to be a woman, anyway?

CONSCIENCE: Ask God.

CONFESSION: What's with you? Do your part and stop getting off the script. We'll never get finished here. You wanted the role of Everyman. You're the only man that showed up when we had auditions, anyway.

EVERYMAN: Yeah.

CONSCIENCE: We could have cast a woman and called it Everywoman.

CONFESSION: Can we get back to it?

EVERYMAN: I'm not kneeling.

CONFESSION: Okay. Don't kneel.

CONSCIENCE: I think he should kneel. After all he is confessing his sins.

CONFESSION: It would make it more real to you. You would get into it more. You might even feel repentant.

EVERYMAN: Who asked you anyway, Conscience? Why don't you just butt out.

CONFESSION: Now don't talk to her that way. You know she's helped you with your lines.

EVERYMAN: You're always insulting my intelligence. Don't you think I know what I'm doing?

CONSCIENCE: I don't think you want an honest answer to that.

EVERYMAN: I wouldn't get it from you anyway.

CONSCIENCE: You're an actor. You can't recognize honesty when you see it. You live in a world of fantasy.

EVERYMAN: Listen, who do you think you are, the director? I don't need you. Get lost.

CONSCIENCE: All right. I can see you don't want me.

CONFESSION: We can't do this without you. We need you, Conscience.

EVERYMAN: Speak for yourself.

CONFESSION: I was speaking for you.

EVERYMAN: I can speak for myself without any help, thank you.

CONSCIENCE: You don't really don't want me around?

EVERYMAN: You got it.

CONSCIENCE: Good-bye, then. (*SHE EXITS*)

CONFESSION: Now you've done it. You've lost your conscience.

EVERYMAN: Aw, who needs her anyway. Her part's over.

CONFESSION: And who will give you your lines when you make a mistake?

EVERYMAN: I won't make any.

CONFESSION: We'll see.

EVERYMAN: Yes, we will, won't we.

CONFESSION: All right, say your line. Confess.

EVERYMAN: Uh, give me the line.

CONFESSION: I can't give you the line. I don't know your line. Conscience left with the only script.

EVERYMAN: Never mind. I've got it. "Oh, glorious fountain ..." "Oh, glorious ..." Oh, I can't do it.

CONFESSION: What's your problem?

EVERYMAN: I can't do this play. I wanted to be in a play, not do some stupid mealy-mouth part like this.

CONFESSION: It's a medieval play.

EVERYMAN: It sure is.

CONFESSION: You don't think it speaks to us today?

EVERYMAN: Of course not. How could it? No one confesses anything today. Don't you read the newspapers? The only reason to confess is to plea bargain for a lighter sentence.

CONFESSION: Don't you think people confess to God?

EVERYMAN: I suppose there are a few people. The minister probably does. And I suppose women do.

CONFESSION: But men don't?

EVERYMAN: Why would they? Come to think of it, it is right that you should be a woman, it's a woman's thing to do.

CONFESSION: Let's get on with the play.

EVERYMAN: Why?

CONFESSION: Because we have a performance next week.

EVERYMAN: Let's forget it. I'm tired. And I have a headache. And I don't like this script. (*HE EXITS*)

CONFESSION: Great. Here I am with no one to confess. This happens more than I want to admit. We always have had a hard time filling this role.

The Lord, The Holy Spirit

Theme:
    The baptism of the Holy Spirit for service.

Summary:
    A choral reading. Several renowned Christian leaders speak about their empowering by the Spirit for service.

Playing Time	7 minutes
Place	A neutral reading area
Props	Black folders with scripts
Costumes	Black
Time	The present
Cast	FIRST READER
	SECOND READER
	THIRD READER
	FOURTH READER
	D.L. MOODY
	CHARLES FINNEY
	R.A. TORREY
	CATHERINE MARSHALL

FIRST: (*ENTERS ALONG WITH SECOND, THIRD, AND FOURTH READER*) We are living in the age of the Spirit.

SECOND: Now, concerning matters pertaining to the Spirit, I would not have you ignorant (*1 Corinthians 12:1*).

FIRST SMALL GROUP: A new Spirit will I put within you.

ALL: I will put my Spirit within you (*Ezekiel 36:26, 27*).

FIRST: The Holy Spirit, He is God.

SECOND: We are transformed into the same image from glory to glory, even as from the Lord, the Spirit (*2 Corinthians 3:18*).

THIRD: The Spirit of God has made me and the breath of the Almighty has given me life (*Job 33:4*).

SECOND SMALL GROUP: A new Spirit will I put within you.

ALL: I will put my Spirit within you.

FOURTH: For the law of the Spirit of Life in Christ Jesus has made us free from the law of sin and death (*Romans 8:2*).

SECOND: As God is love, so the Spirit is Truth.

ALL: He shall baptize you with the Holy Spirit and with fire (*Matthew 3:11, 12*).

FIRST: Your body is the temple of the Holy Spirit who is in you (*1 Corinthians 6:19*).

D. L. MOODY: I suppose there is not a real Christian here, today, but has a real desire to be used of God. If you have no desire, no longing for usefulness, I should say there is something wrong in your life. But first, we must know the mind of the Holy Spirit, give ourselves up wholly, to be led and guided and filled with the Spirit.

The Holy Spirit can do more in one day than you and I can in five years. I hope he will come and work in each of our hearts today.

And this is his dwelling place, in these bodies that you and I inhabit. When we have been near the son of God, then it is that these bodies become temples for the Holy Ghost to dwell in. Jesus says, "He shall be in you. He shall abide in you." We have been bought, not by silver, but by the precious Son of God.[1]

FIRST SMALL GROUP: A new Spirit will I put within you.

ALL: I will put my Spirit within you (*Ezekiel 36:26, 27*).

THIRD: Great men of God have been great men of the Spirit.

SECOND SMALL GROUP: Holy men of God spoke as they were moved by the Holy Spirit (*2 Peter 1:20, 21*).

ALL: Francis of Assisi, Martin Luther, Charles Wesley ...

FOURTH: Charles Gradison Finney.

FINNEY: I had recently accepted the gospel salvation of Jesus Christ and the thought of God was sweet to my mind and the most spiritual tranquillity had taken full possession of me. This was a great mystery.

This one particular evening I had begun to play my bass-viol and sing some pieces of sacred music and as I began to sing those sacred words, I began to weep. It seemed as if my heart was all liquid. After trying in vain to suppress my tears, I put up my instrument and stopped singing.

There was no fire and no light in the room; nevertheless it appeared to me as if it were perfectly light. It seemed as if I met the Lord Jesus Christ face to face. He stood before me and I fell down at His feet and poured out my soul to Him. I wept aloud like a child, and made such confessions as I could with my choked utterance. It seemed to me that I bathed His feet with my tears.

It was then that I received a mighty baptism of the Holy Ghost. Without any expectation of it, without ever having the thought in my mind that there was any such thing for me, without any recollection that I had ever heard the thing mentioned by any person in the world, the Holy Spirit descended upon me in a manner that seemed to go through me, body and soul.

No words can express the wonderful love that was shed abroad in my heart. I wept aloud with joy and love; and I do not know but I should say, I literally bellowed out the unutterable gushings of my heart.

I continued in this state for quite a long time until I was interrupted by one of my choir members, for I was then the leader of the choir. He entered and seeing me in this state of loud weeping, said to me, "Mr. Finney, what ails you? Are you in pain?" I could not answer him for quite some time but gathered myself up the best I could and said, "No, Sir, but so happy that I cannot live."

He turned and left the office and soon returned with one of the church elders. This elder was a very serious man, and I had scarcely ever seen him laugh. When they both entered I was still weeping and the elder asked me how I felt and I began to tell him and at this time he fell into a most spasmodic laughter. It seemed as if it was impossible for him to keep from laughing from the very bottom of his heart.

There was a young man in the neighborhood who was unconverted and as the precise moment was entering our office and upon hearing my weeping confessions and the laughter of the sober elder, threw himself on the floor and cried out with the greatest agony of mind, "Do pray for me!" We all prayed for him and he, too, accepted the salvation of Jesus Christ. This is the manner in which I was baptized with the Holy Ghost.[2]

FOURTH: Dwight L. Moody.

MOODY: My encounter with the Holy Spirit was much the same as yours, except my experience came long after I was born again and in fact I was quite well known and was having great success as an evangelist. Great crowds were coming to the tabernacle in Chicago, but I was a great hustler and was doing the work largely in the energy of the flesh.

It so happened that two humble Free Methodist women, Auntie Cook and Mrs. Snow, used to attend these meetings quite regularly and sit on the front row. I couldn't help seeing that they were praying during most of my services. Finally I spoke to the women about it.

They said they had been praying for me. "Why me?" I asked, a bit nettled. "Why not the unsaved?"

"Because you need the power of the Spirit!" was their answer.

They continued on in their prayers and after some weeks I invited them to my office one day to talk about the power of the Spirit. "You spoke of the power for service," I reminded them. "I thought I had it. I wish you would tell me what you mean." So the two women told me all they knew about the baptism of the Holy Spirit and then they left.

From that very hour there came a great hunger in my soul. I really felt that I did not want to live if I could not have this power for service.

Then, later that same year I was in New York, preparing to leave for England, when suddenly, as I was walking up Wall Street, in the midst of bustling crowds, my prayers were answered; the power of God fell on me so overwhelmingly that I knew I must get off the street. I saw a house I recognized and knocked on the door and asked if I might have a room by myself for a few hours. Alone there, such joy came upon me that at last I had to ask God to withhold His hand lest I die on the spot from the very joy.

My sermons weren't that changed after the incident, but there was a definite change in the response. People were stirred by the ministering of the Holy spirit and hundreds responded to His wooing. And I would not be placed back where I was before that blessed experience if you should give me all the world.[3]

FOURTH: R. A. Torrey.

TORREY: Remember, D. L., I told you about my baptism; it was quite different from either of your experiences. There was a time in my ministry when I was led to say that I would never enter my pulpit again until I had been definitely baptized with the Holy Spirit and knew it.

I shut myself up in my study and day by day waited upon God for the baptism with the Holy Spirit. It was a time of struggle. The thought would arise, "Suppose you do not receive the baptism with the Holy Spirit before Sunday. How will it look for you to refuse to go into the pulpit?" But I held fast to my resolution. I had in mind what might happen when I was baptized with the Holy Spirit, but it did not come that way at all. One morning as I waited upon God, one of the quietest and calmest moments of my life, it was just as if God said to me, "The blessing is yours. Now go and preach." If I had known my Bible then as I know it now, I might have heard that voice the very first day speaking through the Word, but I did not know it and God in His infinite mercy, looking upon my weakness, spoke it directly to my heart. There was no particular ecstasy or emotion, simply the calm assurance that the blessing was mine.

Some time passed, I do not remember just how long, and I was sitting in that same study, I do not remember that I was thinking about the subject at all, but suddenly it was just as if I had been knocked out of my chair onto the floor, and I lay upon my face crying, "Glory to God! Glory to God!" I could not stop. Some power, not my own, had taken possession of my lips and my whole person. Now, I'm not of an excitable, hysterical or even emotional temperament, but I lost control of myself absolutely. I had never shouted before in my life, but I could not stop.

This last experience was interesting, of course, but I tell you this to emphasize the fact that the moment that I was baptized was not in that moment of ecstasy but in that calm hour when God said, "It is yours. Now go and preach."[4]

SECOND: The wind blows where it will, and though you hear its sound, yet you neither know from where it comes nor where it goes. So it is with everyone who is born of the Spirit (*John 3:8*).

FIRST: The Holy Spirit has not been poured out on you or me to prove how great we are, but to prove the greatness of the son of God.

FOURTH: Catherine Marshall.

MARSHALL: At the time of my baptism in the Holy Spirit I had no group to lay hands on me. Very quietly and undramatically I asked for the gift of the Spirit. The setting was my bedroom with no other human being present.

Scripture makes it clear that the Holy Spirit is not fond of spectacular ways of exhibitionism. After all, no trumpets herald the pinky-gray dawn. No bugles announce the opening of a rosebud. God speaks not in thunder or in the roaring wind, but rather in a still small voice.

So I knew I should guard against demanding a highly emotionally or dramatic experience as initial proof of my baptism in the Spirit. Our triumphant Lord does not need to prove anything. If Jesus wanted to grant me some dramatic evidence, fine, but I would wait for His timing.

Nothing overt happened the first day. I experienced no waves of liquid love or ecstatic joy. But in the next few days, quietly but surely, the Holy Spirit made known His presence in my heart. Day by day came the evidence that after I had asked the Spirit to enter and take charge he had done exactly that.[5]

THIRD: What father among you, if his son asks for a loaf of bread, will give him a stone; or if he asks for a fish, will give him a serpent? If you, then, being evil, know how to give good gifts to your children, how much more will your Father give the Holy Spirit to those who ask Him (*Luke 11:11-13*).

SECOND SMALL GROUP: A new Spirit will I put within you.

ALL: I will put my Spirit within you.

THIRD: I bow my knees before the Father.

FIRST: That He would grant you, according to the riches of His glory, to be strengthened with power through His Spirit in the inner man (*Ephesians 3:14-16*).

TORREY: Do you remember that afternoon in Northfield, D. L.? It was a students' convention. I had spoken that morning in the church on how to receive the baptism with the Holy Spirit. As I drew to a close I noticed it was about noon. You had invited us all to go up the mountain that afternoon at three o'clock to wait upon God for the baptism with the Holy Spirit. But I said to them, "Gentlemen, it is exactly twelve noon and Mr. Moody has invited us to go up the mountain at three o'clock to wait upon God for the baptism with the Holy Spirit. Some of you cannot wait three hours, nor do you need to wait. Go to your tent, go to your room, go into the woods, go anywhere where you can get alone with God, meet the conditions of the baptism with the Holy Spirit and claim it at once."

At three o'clock we gathered; four hundred fifty-six of us. And one after another perhaps seventy-five men arose and said, "I could not wait until three o'clock. I have been alone with God and I have received the baptism with the Holy Spirit." Then you said, "I can see no reason why we should not kneel and ask God that the Holy Spirit may fall on us as he fell on the apostles at Pentecost." We knelt down on the ground; some of us lay on our faces on the pine needles. And we prayed.

A cloud gathered over the mountain, and as we began to pray the cloud broke and the raindrops began to come down upon us through the overhanging pine trees, but another cloud, big with mercy, had also rained on us and we never forgot it.[6]

FIRST SMALL GROUP: A new Spirit will I put within you.

ALL: I will put my Spirit within you.

FIRST: The counselor, the Holy Spirit, whom the Father will send you, in my name, He will teach you all things, and bring to your remembrance all that I have said to you (*John 14:26*).

---

1. Richard S. Rhodes, ed., *Moody's Latest Sermons* (Chicago: Rhodes and McClure Publ. Co., 1898), pp. 447, 455.

2. Helen Wessel, ed., *Autobiography of Charles G. Finney* (New York: Fleming H. Revell Co., 1876), pp. 19, 21, 23.

3. William R. Moody, *The Life of D. L. Moody* (New York: Fleming H. Revell Co., 1900), pp. 146, 147, 149; and R. A. Torrey, *Why God Used D. L. Moody* (New York: Fleming H. Revell Co., 1923), pp. 51-55.

4. R. A. Torrey, *The Person and Work of the Holy Spirit* (New York: Fleming H. Revell Co., 1910), pp. 243-245.

5. Catherine Marshall, *The Helper* (Carmel, N. Y. : Guideposts 1978), pp. 66, 67.)

6. Torrey, *The Person and Work of the Holy Spirit*, pp. 245, 246.

The Lesser Commission

Theme
Doubting what the Lord says is not a recent phenomenon.

Summary
Three disciples meet Jesus and Jesus gives them the "great commission" but they are slow to hear and immune to learning.

Playing Time	3 minutes
Setting	A mountain in the Holy Land
Props	None
Costumes	Disciples — contemporary
	Jesus — Jesus robe
Time	A time with Jesus
Cast	MATTHEW — a follower of Jesus
	THOMAS — also a follower of Jesus
	JOHN — him too
	JESUS

MATTHEW: (*ENTERS WITH THOMAS AND JOHN*) Jesus told us to meet Him here.

THOMAS: But why here, Matthew? Why on a mountain?

MATTHEW: I don't know.

JOHN: We must learn to do as He says, that's all.

MATTHEW: Yes, you're right, John. You're right.

THOMAS: I mean to have more faith in the Master. I have doubted in the past, but that is going to change.

JOHN: I hope it does, Thomas. I hope we all can change when it comes to having faith.

JESUS: (*ENTERS*) Thank you for being faithful and meeting me. (*THE DISCIPLES WORSHIP JESUS*)

THOMAS: My Lord and my God.

JESUS: (*AS JESUS SPEAKS DISCIPLES FREEZE THROUGH-OUT*) All authority has been given to me in heaven and on earth.

THOMAS: (*THEY UNFREEZE AS THEY SPEAK*) Wait! Stop! What did He say?

JESUS: All authority has been given to me in heaven and on earth.

THOMAS: I doubt if He means all authority.

MATTHEW: He certainly must mean something else.

JOHN: Maybe He means "quite a lot of authority has been given to me since I rose from the dead." That would sound better.

MATTHEW: Yes, it would sound better. Who would believe it if He said all authority?

JOHN AND THOMAS: No one.

MATTHEW: Right.

JOHN AND THOMAS: Right.

JESUS: All authority has been given to me in heaven and on earth.

THOMAS: Hold it! Hold it!

JESUS: All authority has been given to me in heaven and on earth.

THOMAS: Do you think He means on earth as well as heaven?

MATTHEW: I see what you mean. He couldn't mean on the entire earth.

JOHN: It's easy for me to believe He has authority in heaven. He is the Son of God, but not on earth. Just look at the earth. It's in pretty bad shape.

MATTHEW: I'll say. He probably means He has some limited authority on earth as a representation of the authority He has in heaven.

JESUS: Go, therefore and make disciples of all nations baptizing them in the name of the Father and the Son and the Holy Spirit.

THOMAS: Whoa! What was that?

JESUS: Go, therefore and make disciples of all nations baptizing them in the name of the Father and the Son and the Holy Spirit.

MATTHEW: What do you think? He probably means for us to support each other and the people who don't believe as we do will learn from what we do.

JESUS: Go, therefore and make disciples of all nations baptizing them in the name of the Father and the Son and the Holy Spirit.

JOHN: He can't possibly mean we should baptize like John did in the wilderness.

MATTHEW: That's probably symbolic.

THOMAS: Let's not get into the baptizing question. You know how we had that big fight the last time He brought that up.

JOHN: That's right. I doubt if He means we should fight about it.

THOMAS: So He probably meant it to be symbolic like Matthew says.

JESUS: Go, therefore and make disciples of all nations baptizing them in the name of the Father and the Son and the Holy Spirit.

MATTHEW: Right. And what about that last part: in the name of the Father and the Son and the Holy Spirit. What is that?

JOHN: A formula. Simply a formula.

THOMAS: (*NOT REALLY UNDERSTANDING*) Oh, yeah.

JESUS: Teaching them to observe all that I commanded you; and lo, I am with you always, even to the end of the age.

JOHN: What was that? What did He say?

JESUS: Teaching them to observe all that I commanded you; and lo, I am with you always, even to the end of the age.

JOHN: I doubt if He means *all* that He commanded us. That's quite a lot. I suppose if all the commands were written down it would fill the whole world.

MATTHEW: How can He be with us always? I admit it would be nice, but always? Let's get serious.

THOMAS: Even to the end of the age? What does that mean? I doubt if He means this present age.

JOHN: Do you know something, I think we have voiced some serious doubts about what He said.

MATTHEW: Hey, you know, you're right. We have voiced some serious doubts.

THOMAS: I doubt if Jesus would want us to have doubts.

MATTHEW: I doubt it too.

JOHN: I doubt if He wants us to continue doing this.

THOMAS: Doing what?

JOHN: Doubting, Thomas.

THOMAS: Oh, yeah.

MATTHEW: Well, what then?

THOMAS: What do we do?

JOHN: I doubt if Jesus would want us to doubt at all.

MATTHEW: I doubt it.

THOMAS: I really doubt it.

JOHN: I doubt it, too. (*THE DISCIPLES EXIT*)

JESUS: I doubt if they understand.

AIDS

Theme
Believers stumble too. How does a believer handle that?

Summary
A husband and wife deal with the news that the husband is HIV positive.

Playing Time	3 minutes
Setting	Their home
Props	None
Costumes	Contemporary
Time	The present
Cast	MARY — married a few years
	ERIC — her husband

MARY: (*FIXING DINNER AS ERIC ENTERS*) You're late.

ERIC: I know.

MARY: Dinner's ready. We'll have to hurry to get to church.

ERIC: Sure.

MARY: What's wrong? Something at work?

ERIC: No.

MARY: Well, what is it then?

ERIC: It's, ah ...

MARY: What?

ERIC: Bill Hartley called me today.

MARY: Dr. Hartley, what did he want? Was it about your exam? Are you all right?

ERIC: I'm fine. Well, no, I'm not. Not really.

MARY: What is it? What's wrong?

ERIC: Bill ask me to drop by after work to see him. That's why I was late getting home.

MARY: What is it?

ERIC: He wanted to talk to me.

MARY: What do you mean?

ERIC: It's pretty serious, really.

MARY: What? What is it?

ERIC: It was the blood test. It came back from the lab and he wanted to talk to me about it.

MARY: Eric, what is it?

ERIC: Bill said I tested HIV positive.

MARY: What?

ERIC: HIV positive. I have the HIV virus.

MARY: No!

ERIC: Yes. Yes, I do.

MARY: Is he sure?

ERIC: I asked him the same thing. Yes, he's sure.

MARY: You've got AIDS!

ERIC: Well, not really, no.

MARY: What do you mean, not really? Of course you do. It's A.I.D.S.! That's what it means, doesn't it? You've got AIDS!

ERIC: No, it doesn't mean that. I've read about it. It means it's possible I might get AIDS someday.

MARY: I've read a lot about it, too. And I know one thing — you can give it to me. If I have it I can give it to any babies I have. Eric, AIDS!

ERIC: Bill suggested you come in for a blood test, too.

MARY: We can't have children now. Why? Why?

ERIC: Mary, it will be all right.

MARY: All right? What are you talking about? Our entire life is changed. Changed in an instant. Why?

ERIC: (*TRYING TO COMFORT HER*) Mary.

MARY: Oh, leave me alone. AIDS! You've got AIDS!

ERIC: Mary, please.

MARY: Leave me alone.

ERIC: I've been trying to tell you, Bill said the actual disease might never develop. If it does it might be five or ten years from now. We just have to hope for the best.

MARY: The best? There is no best now. Not now. Never again. Why, Eric? Why?

ERIC: Mary, please. I'm sorry. Please try to understand.

MARY: AIDS!

ERIC: I don't have AIDS!

MARY: As far as I'm concerned, you've got it.

ERIC: Mary, you don't understand.

MARY: I understand very well. You've got AIDS and you know it. I've probably got it too, I just don't know about it yet.

ERIC: I wish it had never happened. All those ... I just didn't know. I just never thought it would lead to this.

MARY: Why didn't other doctors find it? Maybe Dr. Hartley made a mistake.

ERIC: There was no mistake. He took two separate samples. There was no mistake. I wish there was.

MARY: There was a mistake. Our marriage was a mistake. We can never have children now.

ERIC: I know. I know. I'm so sorry.

MARY: What are we going to do? I just don't know what we're going to do. What are we going to do? Why, Eric? Why? Why us?

ERIC: I told you all about my life before we got married. I told you.

MARY: I know, but I didn't think it would affect us like this — and our children, or, I mean, oh, it's hopeless. All our dreams. We don't have any more dreams. No more dreams. No more life.

ERIC: Mary, please. We can go on. People do go on. People do.

MARY: Do they? How? Do we? Do we go on? How long? How long do we go on? How long? You said five years — ten years. Year after year waiting for you to get sick or waiting for me to get sick — waiting for one of us to catch pneumonia and die. That sounds like a lot of hope. Is that how people go on? Is it? Well, I can't. I just can't! Why should I? Why should I have to?

ERIC: We can't undo the past. I wish we could.

MARY: So do I.

ERIC: Mary, I love you. Just you. Just you. You know that. You know that for sure.

MARY: I know.

ERIC: (*TAKING HER IN HIS ARMS*) We can make it, Mary. We can make it but we have to know for sure we have each other's love.

MARY: Yes, I know. I do love you, Eric. I do love you.

ERIC: And we know another thing, Mary. We know we have the love of God.

MARY: Yes, but ...

ERIC: What, Mary?

MARY: I just wish you would have met the Lord before ... well, you know.

ERIC: Yes, so do I.

The Inmate

Theme

Turn the other cheek? It sounds good when you read it in the Bible, but is it possible today?

Summary

An inmate in prison is trying to turn the other cheek and is being questioned by the guard commander.

Playing Time	3 minutes
Setting	A prison office
Props	File containing reports, homemade knife
Costumes	Guard, commander — officer uniform, white shirt, black trousers, black tie
	Stinder — Inmate blue work pants, undershirt
Special Makeup	Stinder — Eye patch with dried blood, black eye, other wounds
Time	The present
Cast	GUARD — Captain White
	STINDER — Willie Stinder — the inmate

STINDER: (*ENTERS TO STAND IN FRONT OF GUARD*) My quad commander told me to report to you, Sir.

GUARD: (*LOOKING OVER PAPERS IN FILE FOLDER*) Right. Stinder, I see by your record you've been written up several times and gone to the hole several times.

STINDER: That's correct, Sir.

GUARD: And you've been in a fight again. (*HOLDS HOME-MADE KNIFE*) And this time there was this shiv.

STINDER: Yes, Sir.

GUARD: You know I'm going to send both you and Wiles to the hole.

STINDER: Yes, Sir.

GUARD: This doesn't look good on your record, Stinder. You've had more write-ups than anyone in this entire prison. What's your problem?

STINDER: It's not my problem, Sir.

GUARD: It certainly is your problem. You know the rules — if you're in a fight you get written up. You know this will affect your chance of parole.

STINDER: I thought it would, Sir.

GUARD: What are you going to do about it?

STINDER: I pray a lot about it, Sir.

GUARD: What do you mean?

STINDER: I mean, when I don't know what to do about a problem right away, I pray.

GUARD: Are you religious?

STINDER: I'm a Christian, Sir.

GUARD: Your religion hasn't helped you very much, has it?

STINDER: I think my relationship with Jesus has strengthened me, Sir.

GUARD: How? You're in the hole more than you're out. Somebody could have gotten killed this time, Stinder.

STINDER: I've been able to forgive every man who attacks me.

GUARD: That's commendable, Stinder. How can you stop fighting?

STINDER: Oh, I never fight, Sir.

GUARD: I've got a fist full of reports that says you do.

STINDER: Well, Sir, uh, they're wrong, Sir.

GUARD: Wrong?

STINDER: Yes, Sir. I've been attacked but I never fight back.

GUARD: Do you mean that you never hit back when you're hit? That isn't natural.

STINDER: It's what Jesus said to do, though. He said, "Whoever hits you on your cheek offer him the other also." I try to live by what Jesus said.

GUARD: Yes, Stinder, I understand, but do you see that it is hurting your record?

STINDER: I know that, Sir, but I have to do what Jesus tells me.

GUARD: Can't you avoid these attacks?

STINDER: Can you watch the inmates all the time, Sir?

GUARD: No, we can't.

STINDER: Well, then, there's your answer.

GUARD: What if I post you to other duty, one that is more visible?

STINDER: I'd just as soon stay where I am, Sir.

GUARD: But you'll just get attacked again.

STINDER: Probably so, Sir. I just don't want any favors.

GUARD: I can understand that. But what are we going to do about these attacks on you?

STINDER: There's nothing you can do, Sir.

GUARD: And nothing you will do, right?

STINDER: I have to be true to what I believe, Sir.

GUARD: I understand that. I respect you for it.

STINDER: Maybe there is something you can do, Captain.

GUARD: What is that?

STINDER: You could pray for the guys that attack me.

GUARD: Pray for the other guy? Why don't you ask me to pray for you?

STINDER: You can pray for me too, if you want. But it's the other guys who need it. They need to know Jesus and then they wouldn't attack others, would they?

GUARD: I guess you're right, but ...

STINDER: Do you pray, Captain?

GUARD: Well, no. No, not much.

STINDER: Maybe in your position it would help. I pray for you.

GUARD: Yes, well ... Anyway, Stinder, I have to send you to the hole.

STINDER: I know that, Sir. It's all right. I can still pray in solitary.

GUARD: You'll be taken to solitary tomorrow morning. And, Stinder, get your shirt on. You're out of uniform.

STINDER: Yes, Sir. I know. But I don't have another shirt.

GUARD: Who took your shirt?

STINDER: No one, Sir. Wiles cut himself pretty bad with the knife he had and I bandaged his wound with my shirt.

GUARD: You bandaged the wounds of the man who was trying to kill you?

STINDER: Yes, Sir. Jesus said ...

GUARD: Never mind, Stinder. You're excused. (*STINDER EXITS*)

Fatherhood

Theme
People get their idea of God from their relationship with their fathers.

Summary
Shirley has a mean father and when a friend tries to interest her in Christianity by telling her God is a loving father, she is not interested.

Playing Time	3 minutes
Setting	Shirley's home
Props	A box of candy
Costumes	Contemporary, casual
Time	The present
Cast	SHIRLEY — a teenager
	FATHER — her father
	ROGER — Shirley's brother
	EDITH — Shirley's friend

FATHER: (*ENTERS*) Shirley, where are you? You didn't clean up these dishes.

SHIRLEY: (*ENTERS*) I'm sorry, Dad. I had to finish my homework.

FATHER: I told you to do the dishes.

SHIRLEY: I know, but I have so much to do. My teacher ...

FATHER: I don't care. Do the dishes.

SHIRLEY: Okay.

FATHER: When I tell you to do something I expect you to do it.

SHIRLEY: Okay, Dad.

FATHER: What in the world is the matter with you? Can't you do anything right? Just for that you're grounded for a month. (*HE BEGINS TO EXIT*) I don't know, when I was a kid my dad beat me when I didn't mind. I guess I'm just too easy on them.

ROGER: (*ENTERS WITH BOX OF CANDY*) Hi, Shirley, have you got time to work on Mom's present?

SHIRLEY: Get serious. I've got all the dishes to do and then my homework.

ROGER: Well, gosh, you said you'd help me wrap it and everything.

SHIRLEY: Of course. Just leave it on my bed.

ROGER: Mom'll see it. It's a box of candy.

SHIRLEY: Okay, leave it under my bed then.

ROGER: Good idea. See ya later. I've got a date with Marlene. Dad's letting me have the car. (*HE EXITS*)

SHIRLEY: Yeah, see ya.

EDITH: (*ENTERS*) Hi, Shirley. How ya doing?

SHIRLEY: Not so good. I've just been grounded for a month. and I've got all these dishes to do. And I didn't finish my homework.

EDITH: Things are rough, huh? Well, did you think over what we were talking about the other day?

SHIRLEY: About God and stuff?

EDITH: Yeah. He could help you with your problems.

SHIRLEY: I don't see how anyone could help.

EDITH: God could. He's a loving God ... like a loving father who cares for us when we need it most.

SHIRLEY: A loving father ...?

FATHER: (*ENTERS WITH BOX OF CANDY*) Shirley! What the heck is this? I found it under your bed.

SHIRLEY: I ...

FATHER: Never mind your stupid explanations. Hiding candy so I wouldn't find it, eh? Well, miss smarty pants, you'll find that sneaking around is not the way we do things in this family. (*BE-GINS TO EXIT*) You haven't heard the last of this, young lady.

EDITH: Well, I, ah, you really do need God. He'll love you like a father.

SHIRLEY: No, thanks. I'm not interested.

House On Sand

Theme

The family that fails to build its house on the Rock, Jesus, is heading for some stormy weather.

Summary

Shirley, the daughter, had a bad day at school. Mom had a hard day at home, and Dad comes home tired and out of sorts. There is bound to be an explosion.

Playing Time	3 minutes
Setting	Shirley's home
Props	School books
Costumes	Contemporary, casual
Time	The present
Cast	SHIRLEY — a teenager
	MOTHER — her mother
	FATHER — Shirley's father

SHIRLEY: (*ENTERS AND SLAMS HER BOOKS ON THE TABLE*)

MOTHER: (*SINCE SHIRLEY HAS SPOKEN NO GREETING, MOTHER ACTS IF SHE IS SHIRLEY SPEAKING*) "Hello, Mother, how was your day, Mother?" (*SHE RESPONDS TO HER OWN QUESTION AS HERSELF*) Oh, my day was fine, Shirley. How was your day? (*PLAYING SHIRLEY AGAIN*) "My day was lousy, Mother."

SHIRLEY: Mom, cut it out. I had a bad day. I flunked my test.

MOTHER: You flunked your test! Didn't you study?

SHIRLEY: Of course I studied.

MOTHER: With the television on.

SHIRLEY: I always study with the television on.

MOTHER: When I was young I got good grades and I didn't try to study with the television on.

SHIRLEY: Well, good for you.

MOTHER: Don't you talk to me in that tone of voice, young lady.

SHIRLEY: Lay off, Mother! I've just about had enough. I've had a hard day.

MOTHER: You poor thing. I had a hard day, too. I washed the clothes, mopped the kitchen floor, washed the dishes, which is your job, and to top it off I burned dinner.

SHIRLEY: Knock it off, Mom. I'm going to my room. (*SHE BEGINS TO EXIT*) Oh, by the way, Mom, have a nice day. (*SHE EXITS. MOTHER IS NOW MORE ANGRY THAN SHE WAS*)

FATHER: (*ENTERS. ALSO IN A BAD MOOD. LOOKING IN POT ON STOVE*) What kind of slop is this?

MOTHER: Did you have a bad day, too, dear?

FATHER: Just answer my question. I put up with the dingbat students and the dingbat principal all day. I never get a straight answer to my questions, then I come home to you ...

MOTHER: Are you calling me dingy?

FATHER: Well, you qualify. Now, what is it?

MOTHER: It's chicken.

FATHER: (*MOCKING HER*) "It's chicken." We had chicken last night. We had chicken at school today. I'm up to here with chicken.

MOTHER: Well, the Lord giveth.

FATHER: Well, the Lord can take that away. (*LOOKS IN CUP-BOARD*) Where's the scotch?

MOTHER: You don't need any scotch.

FATHER: Just leave me alone. All I want to do is relax with a little drink and watch some TV. And I don't want to be bothered.

MOTHER: Sure, that's your answer to everything — get a little drink and watch TV.

FATHER: Bug off! (*FATHER IS NOSE TO NOSE WITH MOTHER GLARING ANGRILY AT HER. SHIRLEY STEPS OUT OF THE BEDROOM AND STARES AT THEM*)

Super Christian I

Theme

Well meaning Christians who are not hearing the call of the Lord clearly may do more harm than good and be super-Christians but not really follow God's leading.

Summary

Super Christian, the righter of wrongs, makes a fatal error. He hears a call of distress but makes a quick judgment as to who is the wrong-doer. When asked to do some good himself he has a good excuse.

Playing Time	3 minutes
Setting	Some place near your church
Props	Handbag, Christian tracts
Costumes	Super Christian — a pair of blue pajamas and cape, "S.C." on the chest
Time	The present
Cast	GUY
	GIRL
	ANNOUNCER
	JESUS PERSON
	SUPER CHRISTIAN

ANNOUNCER: (*ENTERS AND SPEAKS INTO MICROPHONE*) Faster than a speeding bullet. Mightier than a mighty locomotive. Able to leap tall church buildings at a single bound.

GUY: Look! Up in the air!

GIRL: It's a bird!

GUY: It's a plane!

ANNOUNCER: No, it's Super Christian! Yes, Super Christian, who, disguised as the mild-mannered Sunday school teacher, wages a never-ending battle for peace, justice, and the Christian way. As our exciting adventure begins two young students from the university are planning their weekend.

GIRL: Hey, why don't you get a six-pack and come on over tomorrow evening.

GUY: Sure, I'll supply the grass.

ANNOUNCER: When suddenly, emerging from a dark alleyway, a figure of questionable repute approaches the couple from the rear.

JESUS PERSON: (*TAPPING GUY ON SHOULDER*) Hello, there.

GIRL: (*SCREAMING*) Help! He's going to steal my purse!

GUY: Hey, what are you up to anyway? (*GUY STRUGGLES WITH JESUS PERSON*)

ANNOUNCER: While not far away, Super Christian's super-hearing ear picks up the distress signal and he flies to the rescue ... very fast.

SUPER CHRISTIAN: (*COMING TO THE RESCUE VERY FAST*) This looks like a job for ... *Super Christian!* (*FLEXING HIS MUSCLES*) You villain of questionable repute. (*KNOCKING JESUS PERSON DOWN*)

GIRL: (*FEELING HIS BICEP*) Oh, thank you, Super Christian. You saved our lives.

GUY: Yes, I don't know what we would have done. I don't know any of the martial arts.

SUPER CHRISTIAN: Are you two all right?

GUY: Yeah, sure.

SUPER CHRISTIAN: Well, take care of yourselves and have a nice and safe and happy weekend.

GIRL: You bet we will. (*THEY BEGIN TO EXIT*) Did you say you were bringing the grass?

SUPER CHRISTIAN: (*PICKING JESUS PERSON UP BY NECK OF SHIRT*) And now for you. It's off to the police.

JESUS PERSON: Wait a minute, Super Christian. I was just doing some street evangelism for Jesus.

SUPER CHRISTIAN: Do you mean you weren't going to rob those young people?

JESUS PERSON: No. I was just going to share God's love with them.

SUPER CHRISTIAN: But my super-hearing ear picked up a call of distress.

JESUS PERSON: All people that don't know Jesus are sending out distress signals. And Jesus loves them all.

SUPER CHRISTIAN: But, I thought ... the way you look ... well, I ... gosh, I'm sorry.

JESUS PERSON: That's all right, Super Christian. Hey, while you're here, why don't you help me distribute these Jesus tracts? You could fly over the city and drop them all around. You could cover much more territory than I could.

SUPER CHRISTIAN: No, I'm afraid I couldn't do that. I have to be ready at a minute's notice to answer any distress call.

JESUS PERSON: Super Christian, we've gathered a warehouse full of food to give to the poor. It's stored in a warehouse not far from here. It has to be delivered to the poor people on the other side of town and we can't get any trucks. You could handle the job in no time.

SUPER CHRISTIAN: Sorry, I have to stay alert just in case a bridge collapses or some other great catastrophe occurs. You never know when I'll be needed.

JESUS PERSON: But, Super Christian ...

SUPER CHRISTIAN: Wait! With my x-ray vision I see a car about to plunge off a cliff. I've got to go. Later! Up, up and away! (*HE EXITS*)

JESUS PERSON: Oh, well. I guess it's up to me.

ANNOUNCER: Tune in next time for another exciting adventure of Super Christian when we'll hear Super Christian say ...

SUPER CHRISTIAN: Who, me, witness? Not on your life!

The Elevator

Theme
Christians are to proclaim the gospel to others, but aren't always faithful to do that. We miss the opportunities set before us.

Summary
Sam and Nancy are in love. Both are Christians but haven't told the other. The elevator on which they are riding gets stuck and may crash. Here is an opportunity to tell the other but they miss it.

Playing Time	7 minutes
Setting	An elevator in a high rise
Props	None
Costumes	Contemporary, casual
Time	The present
Cast	GEORGE
	SAM — his friend
	WOMAN — passenger
	NANCY — Sam's girl
	DARLENE — Nancy's friend

GEORGE: (*ENTERS ALONG WITH SAM, TALKING AS THEY RUN FOR THE ELEVATOR*) Hurry, let's catch this elevator.

SAM: C'mon, I'll hold it.

GEORGE: (*IN THE ELEVATOR*) Well, you have to tell her, you know.

SAM: Yes, I guess I do. But, how?

GEORGE: Boy, is this elevator slow. How? I don't know. Maybe the four spiritual laws or something.

SAM: That's great for street evangelism — strangers — but this is a girl I'm dating, not some stranger. How would it look, we're at the movie, I gently slip my arm around her, draw her closely to me and whisper, "Do you know God loves you and has a wonderful plan for your life?"

GEORGE: This is not just a girl you're dating. You're serious about her. You said so yourself.

SAM: Well, yes, I am serious about her.

GEORGE: All the more reason to talk to her about the Lord. If you're thinking about marriage ...

SAM: Who said I was thinking about marriage?

GEORGE: You said you were serious.

SAM: Well, yes, I am serious about her. (*A WOMAN GETS ON THE ELEVATOR AND NO ONE SPEAKS FOR A WHILE*)

WOMAN: This elevator is sure running slow. (*SHE EXITS*)

GEORGE: Well?

SAM: Well, what?

GEORGE: What about Nancy?

SAM: I said I was serious about her.

GEORGE: Well, if you're serious doesn't that mean marriage?

SAM: Not in my case it doesn't.

GEORGE: Well, then, what are you serious about? Anyway, wouldn't it be the thing to do to tell her about Jesus?

SAM: I don't know. That's tough to do.

GEORGE: How long have you dated Nancy?

SAM: A year. Why?

GEORGE: I don't know. It just seems right for you to tell her, somehow. Why not just start off by telling how you have this great friend — Jesus. Ease into it that way. Share your joy of the Lord. You'll have a better relationship.

SAM: I don't know. It's tough.

GEORGE: Well, this is my floor. Good luck. (*NANCY ENTERS ELEVATOR*) Oh, hi, Nancy. See ya later. (*GEORGE EXITS*)

SAM: Hi.

NANCY: Hi. (*THEY HUG. PAUSE*) I missed you.

SAM: Yeah, me, too.

NANCY: Nice day?

SAM: Yeah. You?

NANCY: Not bad. What are we doing tonight?

SAM: I don't know.

NANCY: What's wrong with this thing?

SAM: I don't know. It's been slow.

NANCY: I'll say it's slow.

SAM: I don't know. What's on TV?

NANCY: Nothing, probably. I thought we could catch a movie or something.

SAM: (*SNEAKING A LOOK IN HIS WALLET*) I don't feel much like a movie.

NANCY: Well, what then?

SAM: I don't know.

NANCY: I don't feel like cooking tonight. Could we go out?

SAM: Yeah, I guess. (*THE ELEVATOR JOLTS TO A STOP*)

NANCY: I think this thing is stuck.

SAM: Yeah, does look like it, doesn't it.

NANCY: Oh, great.

SAM: I'll ring the alarm button.

NANCY: What'll that do?

SAM: I don't know. Maybe someone will hear it.

NANCY: And ...?

SAM: And fix it, I guess.

NANCY: Well, that's kinda scary, right?

SAM: Well, it's not so bad. We're alone.

NANCY: And trapped ... in an elevator ... twenty-seven floors above the ground ... the very hard ground.

SAM: Don't worry. These things won't crash or anything.

NANCY: *(GETTING A BIT SCARED)* Are you sure?

SAM: Sure, I'm sure. That's just in the movies ... and then Charlton Heston comes to rescue us ...

NANCY: But they always die in those movies.

SAM: That's just the point. It's just the movies. It's just make-believe.

NANCY: We couldn't die?

SAM: Not really. They'll get it fixed in a few minutes.

NANCY: I hope so. I'll admit it, I'm scared. *(ELEVATOR LURCHES)* Sam, I am scared, now. Definitely scared.

SAM: *(SHOWING NO COMFORT TO NANCY)* It's all right. I'll see what I can do. *(HE FIDDLES WITH THE DOORS)* Must be something electrical.

NANCY: Yeah, but people die all the time.

SAM: Not in elevators.

NANCY: Don't mention elevators.

SAM: It's all right, Nancy. It's all right. *(SHE BEGINS TO CRY A LITTLE AT FIRST AND THEN MORE AND MORE)*

NANCY: I'm a little scared. I'm sorry. Please, can't you do something? Do something, please! Sam, do something!

SAM: It's all right. Calm down, Nancy. We'll be all right.

NANCY: No, we won't. They don't know we're here. They don't care. No one cares.

SAM: Calm down. For heaven's sake, calm down.

NANCY: No one cares. Sam, no one cares. I can't stand it. I can't stand it any more!

SAM: Will you shut up! You're getting me upset!

NANCY: (*REALLY CRYING NOW*) You don't even care. No one cares. No one.

SAM: Shut up! *Shut up!* (*THEY SIT IN SILENCE APART*)

NANCY: It moved.

SAM: Yeah.

NANCY: It's working again.

SAM: Yeah. It is. (*PAUSE*) Well, here we are. (*THEY STRAIGHTEN THEIR CLOTHES AND FIX THEIR HAIR. DOORS OPEN*)

NANCY: (*EXITS ELEVATOR*) Oh, there's Darlene.

SAM: I'm going to the restroom. I'll be right back.

NANCY: Okay.

DARLENE: Hi, Nancy, were you trapped up there?

NANCY: Yeah. Yeah, we were.

DARLENE: We saw the repairmen working — and the firemen were called, just in case.

NANCY: Yeah, well, we're all right.

DARLENE: Did you get a chance to talk to Sam, yet?

NANCY: No. It's not so easy.

DARLENE: Just share your love of the Lord with him. Tell him how Jesus has moved in your heart.

The Bible Study

Theme

Studying the Bible is important for Christian growth but the Bible student must be willing to learn and obey the truth of God.

Summary

Reggie, pressed into service as the Bible teacher, is no match for the regulars, who are used to tearing apart the teaching and the teacher.

Playing Time	10 minutes
Setting	Someone's home
Props	A Bible for everyone, stools
Costumes	Contemporary, casual
Time	The present
Cast	REGGIE — The study leader
	WENDY
	BILL
	ILKA
	BRUCE
	MAGGIE
	MARK

(THERE IS SOME SMALL TALK AS ALL ENTER)

WENDY: What's the lesson today, Reggie?

BILL: Yeah, it's time to start.

ILKA: Let's begin. This Bible study has become the high point of my week.

BRUCE: Last week's lesson meant so much to me.

REGGIE: My goodness, you sure are anxious. Well, I guess you all know Willie couldn't be here and he asked me to teach the lesson.

BILL: How is he? Has anyone heard?

REGGIE: Well, Rosie said he'd be in the hospital for some time and then he'll need lots of rest.

WENDY: That's terrible.

BRUCE: What's our lesson this week?

REGGIE: Well, Willie told me to teach anything I like so I thought we'd take the tenth chapter of Matthew, verses 32 and 33. Do you all have it? "Whosoever therefore shall confess Me before men, him will I confess also before My Father which is in heaven. But whosoever shall deny Me before men, him will I also deny before My Father which is in heaven." Now as we can see, this is spoken by Jesus to His ...

WENDY: Reggie, excuse me for interrupting, but what translation was that?

REGGIE: That's all right, Wendy. I'm using the King James version. Now, as I was saying ...

WENDY: Do you mind, Reggie, dear, could we hear that read from another version? I don't especially care for the King James version — all those "thees" and "thous."

REGGIE: There aren't any "thees" and "thous" in this passage.

WENDY: I still don't like them.

REGGIE: Well, I don't have another version.

BILL: Here, I do. Want me to read it?

REGGIE: Sure. Go ahead.

BILL: "So everyone who acknowledges Me before men, I also will acknowledge before My Father who is in Heaven; but whoever denies Me before men, I also will deny before My Father who is in Heaven."

REGGIE: Thanks, Bill. Now, as I was saying, Jesus not only speaks to His disciples when He ...

MAGGIE: The word "confess" bothers me.

REGGIE: What's that, Maggie?

MAGGIE: I said, that word "confess." It bothers me.

BRUCE: It doesn't say "confess."

MAGGIE: Of course it does. It says it two times in verse thirty-two.

WENDY: Well, we just read it in that other version, and it said "acknowledge." I like that better.

ILKA: What's wrong with "confess"?

MAGGIE: "Confess." It sounds like Jesus is calling us criminals or something. I don't have anything to confess.

BRUCE: Well, let's use "acknowledge." I can understand that. I mean, I know Jesus, or something like that.

ILKA: That doesn't make sense. "Whosoever therefore shall *know* me before men ..."

MARK: I think of it as recognizing Jesus.

ILKA: "Whosoever therefore shall recognize Me before men ..."

WENDY: It can't mean "recognize." It's like I'm walking down the street and I see Jesus walking my way and I recognize him and say, "Hi, Jesus." Now if there happens to be other people around, then Jesus will do the same for me if I'm in heaven.

REGGIE: I think we should get back to the scripture, folks.

MAGGIE: I still can't stand that word, "confess."

REGGIE: How about "acknowledge"?

MAGGIE: No, I don't like that either.

MARK: I like "recognize."

BILL: How about "identify"?

BRUCE: (*LAUGHING*) "Identify." "Whosoever therefore shall identify Me before men ... No! Can't you see Jesus looking at a police line up. "Yep, that's him, officer."

REGGIE: Now, wait a minute, let's not ...

MARK: Here, let's look it up in the dictionary. Nope, it says "to acknowledge a crime," but here it says "to declare one's faith in."

REGGIE: That's it. To declare your faith in Jesus. You see, if you declare your faith in Jesus ...

BILL: But that doesn't make sense. I mean, the last part of it. Why would Jesus declare His faith in us in heaven?

ILKA: There's one thing that bothers me. This does say,"confess me ..."

BRUCE: (*CORRECTING HER*) "Declares faith in me."

ILKA: All right. All right. That's not the point now. I'm talking about "before *men*."

BILL: So?

ILKA: Oh, you're just like all men. It says "before *men*." Why doesn't it say "before *women*"?

BRUCE: Oh, for Pete's sake.

REGGIE: "Men," as it is being used here, means the universal human race.

ILKA: Of course, but why don't they just say "women" too?

BRUCE: Because it says "men" and any man knows that it means women, too.

ILKA: Well, I want it to say "women."

BRUCE: But we wouldn't want to anger all those men-libbers.

REGGIE: I, ah, think we could easily say "people."

WENDY: Wait. I've got it. We could say "men and women."

REGGIE: "Whosoever therefore shall confess me before men and women"?

BRUCE: Remember, we're using "declare faith in me."

206

REGGIE: Oh, yes, I forgot. I was reading from the Bible. Let's see. "Whosoever therefore shall declare faith in me before men and women."

ILKA: Wait a minute.

BILL: Now, what?

ILKA: Why should women be second?

REGGIE: All right, how about this: "Whosoever therefore shall declare faith in me before women and men."

ILKA: I like that.

BILL: The word we're using now — "faith" — what exactly does that mean?

REGGIE: Faith is belief, trusting, putting your trust in Jesus.

BILL: Yes, I understand. But, "belief," "trust." It's a thing you think. It's in your mind, isn't it?

REGGIE: Yes, it is. When we trust Jesus ...

BILL: Well, if it's a thing you think, how come we do it publicly?

WENDY: Good point. We can't think before women and men. I mean, we can, but how would they know we weren't thinking something else besides that we trust Jesus?

MARK: Good point. People, I mean, "women and men," can't read our minds.

WENDY: It really doesn't make sense.

MAGGIE: It really doesn't.

WENDY: Imagine standing on Main Street and asking "women and men" to read our minds.

REGGIE: I don't think it means that. Let's move on.

MAGGIE: Look, here, it says Jesus will deny us. Why would He deny us if He loves us?

REGGIE: Simply because we have denied Him.

MARK: You mean *if* we deny Him.

WENDY: Deny Him what?

REGGIE: We don't exactly deny Him anything. It's just that we deny that we know Him.

ILKA: Like if we snub Him.

REGGIE: Yes, I suppose. That could be it.

WENDY: If we snub Him He'll do the same before His Father.

ILKA: Let me tell you, my father wouldn't put up with behavior like that. He always taught me to be kind to everyone.

MARK: Wait a minute. This whole thing is wrong. This whole thing. Look at this: "Whosoever shall deny me I will deny." That is flat not biblical. Didn't Jesus say whoever hits you on the right cheek, turn the other cheek?

REGGIE: Yes, He did.

MARK: And didn't He say, if a man, oh, excuse me, if a "woman or man" asks you for your coat, give "her or him" "her or his" coat, too?

REGGIE: Yeah, kinda.

MARK: Then why is He going to snub us?

BILL: Good point. Jesus wouldn't do that.

REGGIE: Well, I think this is a little different ...

MARK: Different? How is it different? He either loves us or He doesn't.

REGGIE: Of course Jesus loves us. But we have to respond to that love. Now, let's get back to our study. "Whosoever therefore ..."

WENDY: I liked the other version better. It didn't say "whosoever" or whatever.

REGGIE: Yes, who read that?

BILL: I did.

REGGIE: Could I use your Bible then, Bill?

BILL: Sure. Here.

REGGIE: "So, everyone who declare faith in Me ..."

MARK: I think we changed that to "trusts or believes," didn't we?

REGGIE: Yes, yes, we did. Let's see now — "So everyone who trusts or believes in Me before women and men ..."

BILL: Didn't we say it was impossible to think before women and men?

REGGIE: We did. Yes, we did. I believe we did. "So everyone ..."

ILKA: Wait, I missed that one. Shouldn't that be ...

REGGIE: Why, yes, you're right. There's one we missed. "So, every woman or man who trusts or believes in Me before." No, I can't say "before," can I?

ILKA: In "her or his" own mind.

MAGGIE: Yes, that's better.

REGGIE: Yes, yes, let's try it again, shall we? "So, every woman or man who trusts or believes in Me in his or her own mind, I also will trust or believe in My mind before My Father who is in heaven."

BRUCE: What do you think? That other part, the part about Jesus denying us — I don't think it's biblical.

MAGGIE: We'll just leave that part out.

REGGIE; We can't do that. This is holy scripture.

WENDY: Well, we could change it, just a little teensy weensy bit, couldn't we?

MARK: Sure, we could. To make it more like Jesus.

ILKA: How about something like the "turn the other cheek" passage?

BRUCE: Yeah. How about something like: "I wouldn't snub you no matter if you snub me or not." Something like that.

REGGIE: Okay, let me see what I've got.

WENDY: Read the whole thing.

REGGIE: Matthew, chapter 10, verses 32 and 33. "So ...

MARK: Do we need that "so" in there. It sounds very demanding.

BILL: No. Cut that out.

REGGIE: Matthew, chapter 10, verses 32 and 33. "Every woman or man who trusts or believes in her or his own mind, I also will trust or believe in my mind. And whatever woman or man who snubs me before women or men, I would never snub before my Father who is in heaven."

WENDY: Very good. I can understand that.

BILL: Me, too. I think that says it all.

BRUCE: Nice study, Reggie. Very worthwhile.

ILKA: Yes, you did very well, Reggie.

MAGGIE: What do we study next week?

MARK: I'm looking forward to it.

REGGIE: I don't know if I can make it next week.

O. J. T.

Theme

There is no peace on earth between the world system and God. They are in constant conflict and taking a stand for the Prince of Peace is often risky. A man's enemies are sometimes masquerading as his friends.

Summary

Ed is told by his supervisor that he is being fired from his job because he will not participate in the training provided by the company.

Playing Time	3 minutes
Setting	A work place
Props	None
Costumes	Business attire
Time	The present
Cast	ED
	JOE — his supervisor

ED: (*ENTERS AND CROSSES TO WHERE JOE IS*) Joe, I'm glad you're here. I wanted to talk to you about the Williams's account.

JOE: I wanted to talk to you, too.

ED: Okay, sure.

JOE: Ed, you've been a good employee in many ways, but I'm going to have to let you go.

ED: Oh, no! Why?

JOE: It's because of your reluctance to participate in our training programs.

ED: I told you I was willing to substitute some other training.

JOE: I told the president that and he said, and I agree with him, that we need a unified training. We can't have people training any way they see fit. That could lead to "Lone Rangers." We have to work as a team.

ED: I can understand that. I am a team member. I work well with all my co-workers.

JOE: But you left the first training session you were in.

ED: Yes, I sure did. I just was not ...

JOE: Well, that doesn't sound like a team player to me. Listen, Ed, I like you but you just don't fit in. Why not give a little bit? I'd like to keep you on. I'm sure we can work something out. I can speak to the president again.

ED: That's fine if you get him to go along with my own training program.

JOE: I told you what he said. He won't change his mind.

ED: Neither will I.

JOE: You're being unreasonable. You're only hurting yourself. Hey, I'm a Christian too, you know. I've been through the training. It's all right.

ED: If you are a Christian you should be the one that is backing me up. That training goes against all the biblical principles that I have been taught.

JOE: We're not training people in the Bible. This is a business, not a Bible school.

ED: My Bible tells me I have to live the Christian life all the time — including my time at work.

JOE: This training goes right along with those Christian principles that you've learned.

ED: No, it doesn't. I just couldn't go along with the training. It was all intended to convince me that I have the power within myself to do anything I want.

JOE: We do have the power within us.

ED: We do.

JOE: There, you see.

ED: We only have that power because God gives us that power.

JOE: Right. There is a God-given power within us.

ED: But you and I are talking about two different things.

JOE: No, we're not. The power within us, that's a God-given thing.

ED: No. If your heart belongs to Jesus the power within you is the Holy Spirit, but if your heart belongs to yourself then the power is from yourself. That power could be used for good or evil.

JOE: Are you saying that the training we are using is evil?

ED: I'm saying it is not of God and I'm saying it's not for me.

JOE: Did you think this was a Christian business when you accepted this job?

214

ED: No. I knew it wasn't. But I didn't think I would be fired because I was a Christian either.

JOE: Listen. I'm a Christian and my job is secure.

ED: But you also go along with whatever they tell you to do. And you don't know your Bible that well. You're not that good a Christian witness.

JOE: I attend church every week. This training has nothing to contradict what is written in the Bible. It has nothing to do with religion.

ED: Don't be too sure of that.

JOE: Where in the Bible does it say anything about this training?

ED: The Bible does say not to worship any other gods.

JOE: You're just a radical.

ED: The Bible also says when humans stop worshiping God they substitute the image of man. And that's what this training does. It substitutes the power of man for the power of God.

JOE: I think you're way off base.

ED: If people rely only on that power within themselves and not God, then who are they answerable to?

JOE: Themselves, of course.

ED: That kinda leaves God out, doesn't it?

ED: It sure does, but I'll tell you again, we're not here to promote God or the Bible.

ED: You don't have to tell me. You're promoting yourself and that's contrary to God's will.

JOE: The training personnel are claiming some pretty impressive statistics.

ED: They certainly are. I've seen them.

JOE: An increase in sales of five percent per month. That's impressive. Less stress. That's impressive. Healing people — they have actually healed people of diseases. Walking on fire — actually walking on fire. That's certainly impressive. Doesn't that sound desirable?

ED: It really does. Any normal person would want this for their company or for themselves, but it accentuates our independence from God and that's the reason I won't participate.

JOE: I think you're being narrow-minded.

ED: I prefer to call it God-centered.

JOE: So, that's your decision, is it?

ED: That's it. I made a decision for Christ many years ago. He's my Lord.

JOE: Do you know how unreasonable you sound?

ED: I'm sticking to my original decision.

JOE: Well, I'm sorry. You're going to lose all your benefits, too, you know. Have you thought about that?

ED: I have. I have to trust the Lord to provide for me.

JOE: You're making the wrong decision.

ED: I don't think so. Joe, you're an intelligent man, why don't you make the right decision and protest this training, too?

JOE: I can't. I have to think about myself.

ED: I know.

The Future Of The Church!
A Speech By Barney Willis

Theme

Sometimes the wise and learned are confounded by spiritual truths and they are revealed to those who are trusting enough to believe Jesus' words.

Summary

Barney Willis, a young college student, is supposed to speak on the "Future of the Church" but can't seem to get started. The reason is revealed by his family.

Playing Time	10 minutes
Setting	Your church
Props	Guitar
Costumes	Contemporary
Time	The present
Cast	BARNEY WILLIS — a college student
	REV. WILLIS —his father
	MRS. WILLIS — Barney's mother
	RUTH WILLIS — Barney's sister.

BARNEY: (*ENTERS WITH GUITAR AND CROSSES TO CENTER STAGE. RETURNS TO GET STOOL AND RETURNS TO CENTER. SITS ON STOOL AND STRUMS*) I don't know what to tell you. I'm not a singer. Can't even play this thing, really. I do this for my own entertainment. You know, it helps to pass the time. I'm in college. I don't have a major yet. What I mean is, not really. Not now. I've got several majors, really. I just can't seem to get interested in any of them. You know. But what I mean is, I really get interested in something but it doesn't last long, you know. I really admire someone who has a major. I'm a senior, or at least I should be. I really was supposed to have graduated a year ago, but with changing majors and all, well, I kinda got messed up somewhere, you know. I really don't think I want to graduate anyway. I don't know what I want to be. You know. (*HE STOPS STRUMMING*)

Hey, let me tell you why I'm here. I'm supposed to talk to you about the future of the Church. (*HE STRUMS AWHILE AND THEN STOPS*) "The Future of the Church!" (*LONG PAUSE. HE STRUMS AGAIN*)

Why me? I just can't seem to get started, you know. Hey, I bet you didn't expect to see me up here playing a guitar, huh? Well, I didn't either, but the guitar makes me feel better. I can sorta hide behind it, you know. I guess I was asked to speak about the future of the church because I'm a religion major, among other majors. Or at least I was a religion major. Officially I still am. But I decided to change. Anyway, as far as the computer at school is concerned, I still am — a religion major, that is. Anyway, I was asked to speak here, before I decided to drop religion, as a major, that is.

Well, here goes: (*HE STOPS STRUMMING*) "The Future of the Church!" (*LONG PAUSE. HE STRUMS AGAIN*)

Hey, I forgot to tell you my name. It's Barney Willis. My nickname is "Slice." I used to run track. In high school, not college. The guys on the team gave me that name. It was meant as a compliment at the time. Now I don't know. I suppose I should get to my speech. It's not very interesting.

Oh, well, here goes: (*HE STOPS STRUMMING*) "The Future of the Church!" (*LONG PAUSE. HE STRUMS AGAIN*)

You know, I wasn't even supposed to make this speech, but Dr. Barlow, he's head of the religion department, he asked me. It seems that the singing Hunters couldn't make it. He said a cold has got most of them. You know how a cold goes through a family. Especially traveling in that bus, or camper, or whatever it is. I felt quite proud to be asked. To replace the singing Hunters, that is. I saw them once in Pittsburgh. They were holding a whole week of meetings. I even heard the five-year-old preach. Pretty good. (*HE STOPS STRUMMING*)

It was right after that I got to thinking about changing my major. (*LONG PAUSE. HE STRUMS AGAIN*) Five years old. Really preached. Sang too. I can't do either very well. But here I am. (*HE STOPS STRUMMING*) Funny when you think about it. I'm replacing a singing and preaching five-year-old with a cold. (*LONG PAUSE. HE STRUMS AGAIN*)

You know something? I know a lot of preachers that act like they're five years old. Well, never mind. Let's get on with it. (*HE STOPS STRUMMING*) "The Future of the Church!" (*LONG PAUSE. HE STRUMS AGAIN*)

It is important, isn't it? The Church, I mean. Well, isn't it? I don't know. My father, he's a minister, he always says it's important.

REV. WILLIS: (*ENTERS AND STANDS APART AS IF IN BARNEY'S MEMORY. BARNEY STOPS STRUMMING*) The church is important, Barnabas. (*HE STRUMS AGAIN*) The Church is an institution, Barnabas, and it will continue to be a vital force in the world. As an institution of great significance it helps to strengthen the lives of millions of people ... Now, Barnabas, about your grades ... (*BARNEY STOPS STRUMMING*)

If you don't improve those grades, Barnabas, I'll have to take some drastic steps to help you. (*PAUSE*) Barnabas, are you listening to me? Well, why don't you say something? (*PAUSE*)

Barnabas, do you realize I'm the pastor of a twelve hundred member church? I doubled the membership of that church in ten years. And as their spiritual father I can talk to any one of them about their religious life. They all respect me. Why? Because they realize that I have the training and the background that can demand respect. The experience I've had proves that I know what I'm talking about. Do you know, Barnabas, that I have three degrees? That means something. I counsel people who come to me with various and sundry problems and I solve those problems for them. It's what I've been trained to do. Now tell me, Barnabas, with all this knowledge and experience and success that I have attained, why is it I cannot talk to you? (*HE STRUMS AGAIN*) Will you cease that stupid playing! You know it makes me nervous. (*BARNEY STOPS STRUMMING*)

Thank you. Now, about those grades, Barnabas, they are not up to the standards that your mother and I have set for you. When I went to school, as you know, I was Phi Beta Kappa. I was also president of my fraternity and as you know, I was an outstanding athlete. Now, at the same time I was engaged in youth work for the Church. I was doing my part, Barnabas. Can you honestly say the same about your own contribution to society? Can you? Of course you can't. Your mother and I want to be proud of you, Barnabas, but we cannot be proud of you if you aren't someone to be proud of, can we? (*PAUSE*)

Barnabas, look at your brother, Jerome. Now, there's a son your mother and I can be proud of. I know you are proud of him too, aren't you? (*HE STRUMS AGAIN*)

Your brother has taken a firm grasp on his life, Barnabas, and is moving toward a great future in the Church. He now has his own church and I'm sure will do great things and have a long and profitable career. We want to be proud of you in the same way, Barnabas. You want to be successful, don't you? Of course you do. Well, you have to get those grades up. Study. Apply yourself. You can be successful like I am. Like Jerome. The Church has a future, Barnabas, it certainly does and your career in the Church can be just as successful. (*PAUSE*)

Barnabas, what did you ever lack as a child? I provided all you ever needed and wanted. I was a success in my field. What did you ever lack? (*REV. WILLIS EXITS. BARNEY STOPS STRUMMING*)

BARNEY: What did I ever lack? I don't know. I really don't know. I can't put my finger on it ... (*HE STRUMS AGAIN*) ... but something. Well, anyway, you see, my father thinks the Church is important. I don't know. It is important to him. I just couldn't get interested. Anyway, I have to start this speech. (*BARNEY STOPS STRUMMING*) "The Future of the Church." Do you know what? I'm not doing so well up here ... (*HE STRUMS AGAIN*)

Aw, shoot, the head of the religion department knew I wouldn't do so well, I guess. I'm doing as well up here as I do in class. Anyway, I guess the Church is growing. I mean, isn't it? It must be, my mom is so busy with her work ... her church work. Well, I guess it must be growing.

MRS. WILLIS: (*ENTERS AND STANDS APART. BARNEY STOPS STRUMMING*) Not now, Barnabas, dear, I'm going to be late for the luncheon. Now, where is my appointment book? I think I have something for tonight, but I can't remember what it is. Well, I'll just have to look for it later.

Good-bye, Barnabas, If you want something to eat it's in the refrigerator. Maybe some of that leftover lamb ... (*SHE EXITS. HE STRUMS AGAIN*)

BARNEY: That's my mom. Leftover lamb. She's very busy, as you can see. So, as I was saying, that must be an indicator of the growth ...

MRS. WILLIS: (*YELLING FROM OFFSTAGE*) Barnabas! (*BARNEY STOPS STRUMMING. MRS. WILLIS REENTERS*) Barnabas, I almost forgot, if Mary calls, tell her that the sloppy joes are all right for Friday night. Bye. (*SHE EXITS. HE STRUMS AGAIN*)

BARNEY: Mary who? Oh, I guess any Mary who calls. Anyway, you can see what I mean. She is busy. So, that must mean that the Church is growing, right? It's growing all right. You should hear my dad. (*REV. WILLIS ENTERS*) Oh, I forgot. You already have. We don't want to go through that again, do we. (*REV. WILLIS EXITS*) I've got to do my talk. (*BARNEY STOPS STRUMMING*) "The Future of the Church."

It's funny, when I was preparing this speech, I got to wondering, does the Church have a future? I wonder ... (*HE STRUMS AGAIN*) I was thinking ... maybe the only reason the Church has lasted as long as it has is that people that make their living at it, I mean the ministers and others, well, maybe they keep it going just so they can continue to make their living.

RUTH WILLIS: (*ENTERS WISTFULLY HUMMING A TUNE*) Hi, Barn.

BARNEY: Hi, Ruthey. (*HE STOPS STRUMMING*)

RUTH WILLIS: Whatcha doin'? Practicin' a new song?

BARNEY: Very funny. You know I can't play.

RUTH WILLIS: Well, what then?

BARNEY: Well, I was just thinking about the Church.

RUTH WILLIS: You know what? I just made up a new song. Want to hear it?

BARNEY: Of course.

RUTH WILLIS: You know, Barn, if you ever learn to play that thing, you can play my songs.

BARNEY: Maybe some day I'll take lessons.

RUTH WILLIS: You could play and I could sing.

BARNEY: Let's hear your song.

RUTH WILLIS: It goes like this:
    There is light,
    In heaven there is light;
    There is light,
    In heaven there is light.

BARNEY: That's nice Ruthey, but ...

RUTH WILLIS: There's more. It's got two parts to it. The other part goes like this:

Jesus, Jesus is the light.
He's the light.
Jesus, Jesus is the light.
He's the light.
Then you put the two parts together. Let's you and I do it, okay?

BARNEY: All right. (*THEY MAKE A FEW ATTEMPTS, BARNEY FOLLOWING RUTH'S LEAD AND THEN FINALLY GET IT RIGHT*)

RUTH WILLIS: That's fun.

BARNEY: I like it, Ruthey. It's so easy, and it's very pretty. I've got to get back to work.

RUTH WILLIS: Homework?

BARNEY: No. Just trying to get my thoughts in order.

RUTH WILLIS: You're not getting like Daddy, are you?

BARNEY: I don't know. What do you mean?

RUTH WILLIS: I mean, whenever I want to talk to him he's trying to put his thoughts in order. Just don't get like him, that's all. See ya later. I've got another verse. (*SHE EXITS. HE STRUMS AGAIN*)

BARNEY: Well, I better get back to it. Uh, well, here goes ... (*HE STOPS STRUMMING*) "The Future of the Church." Normally I would have something to say, but I just can't seem to get started.

What can I say? I suppose you're getting a little impatient with me. I wouldn't blame you if you wanted to leave. I'll guarantee you I've wanted to leave ever since I got here. If you want to leave, just slip out. No one will mind. Certainly not me. I won't tell a soul.

Maybe there's not much to say about the future of the Church. I've got this friend. He dropped out of school and now he's a park ranger. He loves it. Close to nature and all that. He says he's close to God. Well, anyway, he goes to this church and the people just love each other. Nothing special about it, not big or anything, but the people take care of each other and they honor Jesus. It's nice. Maybe I'll visit sometime. Who knows?

RUTH WILLIS: (*ENTERS*) Hi, Barn. You still here?

BARNEY: Sure. Some of the audience left, though.

RUTH WILLIS: Here's the other verse.

BARNEY: Let's hear it.

RUTH WILLIS: There is a love,
On earth there is a love,
There is a love,
On earth there is a love.
Let's sing it together. Want to?

BARNEY: You bet. (*THEY DO AND IT SOUNDS GOOD*)

BARNEY: I like it, Ruthey, but I want some time ...

RUTH WILLIS: To get your thoughts together. Come on, Barn, I want to sing. I want you to sing with me.

BARNEY: But, Ruthey, look at all those people out there. They came to hear me speak about the future of the Church, and they're still here. I can't let them down.

RUTH WILLIS: Well, hurry up and do it then, and then come sing with me. (*SHE EXITS*)

BARNEY: "The Future of the Church." I'm tired of talking about it. I want to go do something about it. (*AFTER BARNEY EXITS WE HEAR RUTH AND BARNEY SINGING TOGETHER*)

The Sower And The Seed And So What

Theme
The word of the Kingdom of God needs to be sown whether we know the outcome or not.

Summary
Ma and Pa are sitting on the porch of their mountain home discussing planting. A parable.

Playing Time	2 minutes
Setting	The porch of Ma and Pa
Props	Two rocking chairs, overalls to patch, a stick to whittle.
Costumes	Ma — sunbonnet, flour sack dress
	Pa — bib overalls, red long johns
Time	Twilight
Cast	MA — old
	PA — older

MA: (*ROCKING AND SEWING, PATCHING PA'S OVERALLS*) Pa?

PA: (*ROCKING AND WHITTLING*) Yup?

MA: Ya lissnin'?

PA: Yup.

MA: 'Member thet seed ya sowed?

PA: Yup.

MA: Wail, ya're a poor 'scuse fer a fermer, ain't ya?

PA: Nope.

MA: Wha, ya're too. I knewed it afore. Now, everbody thet goes past our ferm is agonna' knew it too. Wha, ya ain't got nary a brain thet ya war born with.

PA: Huh?

MA: I said ... Oh, fergit it. Whar'd ya plant thet seed?

PA: Wail ...

MA: I'll tell ya whar ya planted it. Ya planted it right next ta tha path.

PA: Naw.

MA: Don't argue with me. I knowed ya did. When I went up tha path the chickens was all along thar just a peckin' and a peckin' at it. Wha they was amakin' sech a racket I could hardly read the Sears and Roebuck catalogue. Whad ya do thet fer, anyhow? The sun git to ya? Make ya addle-brained?

PA: Nope.

MA: Musta. Ya sowed some on thet rocky patch aground up back a tha barn, didn' ya? I seen it. And I knewed whet was agonna happen. It grewed up a might but then when the sun got hot at noontime it got all brown-like and up and died. Like to make old Bossy sick. And she's offn her feed anyhow.

227

PA: But ...

MA: Don' ya go abuttin' in. Ya sowed some out by tha well, didn' ya? I seen it. Wha, ya knew thet's whar the briar patch is. Nethin's grewed thar but briars since the day Hiram Jamsin's bull get loosed and was atryin' to git in our barn and up and died of heart failure right smack dab on thet very spot. Are ya plumb loco outa yer gourd?

PA: Nope.

MA: Them briars grewed up and choked them thar seeds. Any dab-blamed fool woulda knowed they would.

PA: Yep.

MA: Wail, wheta ya gotta say fer yerself?

PA: Wail ...

MA: Did ya ever do anythin' right? Wail, did ya?

PA: Yup.

MA: Wail, if ya did I like ta know whet it was.

PA: I up and got hitched ta you.

MA: Now, Pa, this is no time to git frisky. I ain't in a frisky mood. I'm in a serious mood. I want to know whet ya did with tha rest of thet seed.

PA: Sowed it.

MA: Whar? Whar did ya sow it?

PA: On the best land thar is.

MA: Tha bottom land?

PA: Yup.

MA: It'll grow real good thar. As a body sez, it'll grow ahunert, sixty, thirty times as much agin, I reckon.

PA: Yup. I done good, huh, Ma?

MA: Nope, ya didn'! Thet thar's Hiram Jamsin's land. (*SHE RUNS HIM OFF THE PORCH BEATING HIM WITH THE OVER-ALLS SHE WAS PATCHING*) Are ya lissenin'? Them look like ears stuck on ta yer haid.

Showdown

Theme

The Kingdom of God is under constant attack from the forces of the world, the flesh, and the devil but is precious enough to fight for. It may look small but it is mighty with the power of the Lord God.

Summary

The Badlanders are coming to town! That means trouble. Chris, the deputy, is responsible for protecting the town while the Sheriff is away. A Parable in the guise of an old fashioned "Meller."

Playing Time	4 minutes
Setting	An old western town
Props	Assorted guns, bull whip
Costumes	Old western. Sheriff — white
Time	Old West
Cast	DOC
	MAYBELLE — a dance hall girl
	BILLY — a young 'un
	CHRIS — deputy (represents the Christian)
	SHERIFF — (represents Jesus)
	MONDO — the world
	CARNEY — the flesh
	DIABLO — the devil

DOC: (*AMBLES IN*) Nice peaceful day. Just a few cow punchers in town after the hard drive. Not much happening.

MAYBELLE: (*RUNNING IN*) Doc! Doc! The Badlands gang is headed for town!

DOC: The Badlands gang!

MAYBELLE: Yup. Cal Snader seen 'em ridin' this way. Near to killed his horse gettin' here to warn us.

DOC: Anyone call the Sheriff?

MAYBELLE: Sheriff's gone. 'Member? What'll we do?

DOC: Tell Chris.

MAYBELLE: Chris Adams?

DOC: Well, he's the deputy, ain't he?

MAYBELLE: But, he's nothin' more than a kid.

DOC: He's still the deputy and he has to know so's he can protect the town.

MAYBELLE: (*SARCASTICALLY*) Protect the town.

DOC: You better hunt him up so's you can tell him.

MAYBELLE: Okay. I'll do it. (*BEGINS TO EXIT*) But, I don't see how he ... (*SHE EXITS*)

DOC: (*TO HIMSELF*) The Badlands gang means trouble. Lots of work for me ... or for the undertaker.

BILLY: (*RUNS IN*) The Badlanders! They're on the way.

DOC: I know. Tell everyone to get off the street.

BILLY: No need. Everybody high-tailed it when they heard the news.

DOC: Where's Chris Adams?

BILLY: The deputy? He's comin' now.

CHRIS: (*ENTERS*) Doc, you better get off the street, too.

DOC: I can still shoot a gun. I'll bet I get a few buttons off the vests of them Badlanders.

MAYBELLE: Chris is right, Doc. You'd better get home. We're going to need you to patch up after the Badlanders leave.

BILLY: What are we going to do, Chris?

CHRIS: Well, Billy, I'm going to warn those Badlanders to be peaceable or move on.

BILLY: Mondo, Carney and Diablo? You're goin' to just warn 'em?

MAYBELLE: Chris, you got to do more than just warn those desparadoes.

CHRIS: I've seen the Sheriff do it plenty of times.

DOC: Sometimes it didn't work though.

CHRIS: But other times it did. Sometimes the trouble makers moved on. Listen, I got to protect this town and I aim to do it.

MAYBELLE: What if they don't move on? What then?

CHRIS: Then I'll have to have them hand over their guns to me.

DOC: Weapons, you mean. Diablo is deadly with a whip. I saw him blind a man once with that thing.

BILLY: There'll be a fight.

DOC: Billy's right, Chris. They ain't peaceable and they never will be.

CHRIS: If it comes to a fight, then I'll fight.

MAYBELLE: You ain't got the experience. Carney wasted a lot of men, I hear tell.

DOC: And Mondo, that fat slob, has killed his share, too. They're a bad lot and us with no Sheriff.

CHRIS: Rest easy, folks. The Sheriff taught me plenty. I can take care of myself and protect this town, too.

BILLY: The Badlanders! They're here! (*EVERYONE COWERS BEHIND CHRIS AS THE BADLANDERS ENTER*)

CARNEY: We're tired and thirsty. Get us a drink! Mondo, you thirsty?

MONDO: Sure am. A double for me.

DIABLO: A whole bottle for me.

MAYBELLE: They'll kill us all.

MONDO: Lookee there, Carney. There's that dame. 'Member the last time? (*LAUGHS*)

CARNEY: Yeah. I 'member. (*TO MAYBELLE*) Hey, you, Missy. Yeah, you. C'mere.

233

MAYBELLE: Chris!

CHRIS: Now, boys, we don't want no trouble here.

CARNEY: Boys? Who's he talkin' to?

MONDO: I dunno. Can't see no boys around here. 'Cept maybe him. (*LAUGHS. DIABLO LAUGHS*) C'mere, Sonny.

CARNEY: Don't you punch him. Let me.

CHRIS: I already told you we don't want no trouble.

CARNEY: (*GRABBING MAYBELLE*) I don't want trouble. I want her. (*HE SLAPS HER AND DRAWS HIS GUN*)

DIABLO: (*GRABBING DOC. MONDO GRABS BILLY*) Now, boys, I guess we'll have things our own way.

CHRIS: I'm ordering you to surrender.

DIABLO: And I suppose you got us surrounded. (*LAUGHS*) I think you're either blind or just plain loco. Don't go for your gun or you're a dead man.

MAYBELLE: Help me! (*CARNEY SLAPS HER.*)

DOC: You best back off, Chris. They've got us. (*THE SHERIFF ENTERS BEHIND THE BADLANDERS HITTING DIABLO ON THE HEAD AND SHOOTING THE OTHER TWO*)

MAYBELLE: (*RUNNING INTO HIS ARMS*) Sheriff! You showed up just in time.

SHERIFF: I've been here all along.

DOC: You have?

SHERIFF: Yep.

BILLY: I didn't know that.

SHERIFF: Chris knew. I was here, but I didn't want the Badlanders to see me until the time was right. Chris, you did a good job.

CHRIS: I couldn't have done it without you.

SHERIFF: Well, rest easy, folks. We'll get this scum locked up. They'll be back, sometime, more than likely, later on, but they know they can't get away with anything in this town.

Before The Wedding

Theme

The kingdom of heaven is like the relationship between a father and daughter. It is a pearl of great price. But sometimes the pearl can be damaged.

Summary

A bride desperately needs to tell her father something that will affect her marriage. The father is slow to hear. A parable.

Playing Time	3 minutes
Setting	The home of the bride
Props	A wedding dress
Costumes	Father — formal suit
	Sue — casual
Time	A few minutes before the wedding
Cast	FATHER
	SUE — the bride

FATHER: (*SUE STANDS, HOLDING HER WEDDING DRESS, WAITING TO BE TAKEN TO THE CHURCH. HER FATHER ENTERS*) Are you about ready, dear? I don't want to rush you, but we are due at the church right now. (*TAKES DRESS*) I'll take that. Your mother is already in the car. You'll go with Billy.

SUE: Can't I ride with you, Daddy?

FATHER: No, honey. It's all been worked out. I'm driving your mother and grandmother. You'll go with your brother. Now, let's get going.

SUE: Daddy, listen to me. I want to ride with you.

FATHER: (*INTENDING TO REASON WITH HER*) Honey ... (*RESIGNING HIMSELF TO IT*) Oh, all right, You can ride with your mother and me. But hurry. Let's go.

SUE: Daddy, wait. You don't understand. I want to be with you ... alone.

FATHER: What?

SUE: I want to talk to you, Daddy.

FATHER: There isn't time, sweetheart. We're due at the church. You are getting married today, you know.

SUE: No. Daddy. Just wait. I want to talk to you.

FATHER: I'm telling you there isn't time!

SUE: DADDY! WAIT! TALK TO ME!

FATHER: Honey, what is it? You're not going to back out of this wedding, are you?

SUE: No. No, I'm not. But I want to tell you something.

FATHER: Sure, honey. I guess we can take the time. It's your wedding.

SUE: Daddy, listen to me. I wanted to tell you this before I married Tom.

FATHER: You love him, don't you?

SUE: Yes, I do. And I love you, too.

FATHER: Honey, it's going to be all right. You're just a little nervous. Tom is a nice man. Your mother and I both like him. You'll raise a nice family. Your mother has always wanted grandchildren. You know how she talks about it. Everything's going to be all right.

SUE: WILL YOU JUST LISTEN TO ME!

FATHER: What is it? What's troubling you?

SUE: Well, first of all, I'm not the innocent girl you think I am.

FATHER: Is that it? Is that what you wanted to tell me? Honey, let me tell you something — don't worry about it. I know young people sleep together these days.

SUE: Please, let me finish. Remember, when I was a freshman and came home because I was so depressed? Remember?

FATHER: Sure, honey.

SUE: I was pregnant. I went to the school counselor and she advised me to get an abortion, so I did.

FATHER: What? What are you saying? You couldn't have. What were you thinking of? You didn't even tell your own mother and father? What were you thinking of?

SUE: I was thinking of my future. At the time I was getting advice from my girlfriends and they said go to the counselor. I needed some advice.

FATHER: What about your parents?

SUE: You were too busy to talk to me, Daddy. I can't ever talk to Mom.

FATHER: But the counselor could have called us.

SUE: Don't you know the law says she doesn't have to tell you if I don't want it? No, I was alone when I made that decision. I was really alone.

FATHER: But, honey, that's all past. This is now and Tom is going to make a good husband and you'll have other children.

SUE: No, Daddy, I won't. That's what I wanted to tell you. I won't ever have children. I can't — a result of the abortion. I just wanted to tell you. You'll have to tell Mom. She won't listen to me.

FATHER: Sue, honey, I, ah, I don't know what to say. I want to help in some way.

SUE: No, not now, Daddy. It's too late. Let's go to the wedding. (*SHE BEGINS TO EXIT*)

FATHER: Wait! Can't we talk?

SUE: We just did. (*SHE EXITS. AFTER A LONG PAUSE HE EXITS*)

Feeding The 4999

Theme

Faith in Jesus is more important than even eating, but He takes care of that need, too.

Summary

Peter is going to try to feed the five thousand without faith so he goes to the nearest fast food restaurant.

Playing Time	4 minutes
Setting	A fast food restaurant
Props	Sam — a microphone, bag of burgers
	Pete — a list
Costumes	Sam — cap and apron
	Pete — disciple
Time	Right before feeding the five thousand
Cast	SAM — clerk at Burger Buddies
	PETE — a customer

PETE: (*SAM STANDS BEHIND THE COUNTER POLISHING THE COUNTER. PETE ENTERS*) Hi.

SAM: Welcome to Burger Buddies. May I help you?

PETE: Do you make up large orders?

SAM: Having a party?

PETE: More like a mob.

SAM: "If it's tough, we can do it!"

PETE: You think you can handle a large order?

SAM: That's our motto. We pride ourselves on doing difficult jobs. "If it's tough, we can do it!" That's our motto.

PETE: I guess I came to the right place.

SAM: You did. "If it's tough, we can do it!" That's our motto, you know.

PETE: I remember.

SAM: How many Burger Buddies do you want?

PETE: Are you ready for this?

SAM: "If it's tough ..."

PETE: "... you can do it!" Right.

SAM: That's our motto.

PETE: I know.

SAM: How many Burger Buddies do you want?

PETE: Four thousand nine hundred and ninety-nine.

SAM: We can't do that!

PETE: What about your motto?

SAM: That's too many! Four thousand nine hundred and ninety-nine. That's too many.

PETE: Your motto. What about your motto? "If it's tough ..."

SAM: We can't do that!

PETE: Wait a minute. Don't get excited.

SAM: Who's excited? You call this excited? We can't do that!

PETE: Just a minute. Now, listen, how many Burger Buddies can you make a minute?

SAM: Top speed?

PETE: The fastest you can make them.

SAM: Let's see — two. Yeah, two a minute. You see, Leo is sick and Willie is a new man on the grill so — yeah, about two.

PETE: Two, huh. Let me see. At that rate, ah, two times sixty is one hundred twenty. And then you divide four thousand nine hundred ninety-nine by one hundred twenty — uh, that's about forty-one hours.

SAM: Forty-one hours!

PETE: Right. I figure it would take about forty-one hours to complete my order.

SAM: Forty-one hours! That's all day. All day and almost two days.

PETE: If you started right now. Did you start my order yet?

SAM: I told you we can't do that. Four thousand nine hundred ninety-nine — forty-one hours.

PETE: Remember your motto.

SAM: Forget the motto.

PETE: This is for a very important person.

SAM: I don't care if it's for the King of Persia.

PETE: It's for Jesus.

SAM: Who?

PETE: Jesus.

SAM: Who?

PETE: Jesus!

SAM: Who?

PETE: It's for Jesus.

SAM: Who?

PETE: JESUS!

SAM: Oh, Jesus. Well, why didn't you say so?

PETE: I did.

SAM: Jesus. That's different.

PETE: All right. Should I come back in a couple of days?

SAM: No. You wait right there. I'll get it for you.

PETE: Huh?

SAM: (*PRODUCING A BAG OF BURGER BUDDIES*) There you go.

PETE: What do you mean?

SAM: Here's your order.

PETE: I ordered four thousand nine hundred ninety-nine Burger Buddies. They'd have to be pretty small to fit in this bag.

SAM: No. No, they don't. Look here. (*OPENING BAG*) There's five buns and two burgers.

PETE: But that's not ...

SAM: That's enough. Take it to Jesus. He'll multiply it.

PETE: Huh?

SAM: Have some faith.

PETE: I do have some.

SAM: Have some more.

PETE: Do you think Jesus can make this into enough food for four thousand nine hundred ninety-nine people?

SAM: Sure. "If it's tough He can do it."

PETE: Hey, that's a good motto. "If it's tough He can do it."

SAM: Sure. "If it's tough He can do it."

PETE: Okay. I'll take it to Him and see what happens.

SAM: Great. See ya.

PETE: What do I owe you?

SAM: Forget it. It's on Burger Buddies.

PETE: Okay. Thanks.

SAM: Remember, "If it's tough He can do it."

PETE: That's our motto.

SAM AND PETE: "If it's tough He can do it."

PETE: (*BEGINNING TO EXIT*) Oh, I forgot. (*TAKING OUT LIST*) I want three hundred without mayonnaise, two hundred twenty-one with onion, three hundred forty-six with just ketchup and pickle ... (*SAM CHASES PETE OFF*)

Water Logged

Theme

If we just trust Jesus He will take care of our needs.

Summary

Peter, the disciple of Jesus, arrives home without a fish for dinner and Ruth, his wife, questions him about it. They will learn a lesson about God's provision.

Playing Time	4 minutes
Setting	The home of PETER
Props	PETER — a fish hidden in Peter's cloak
Costumes	RUTH — cap and apron
	Peasants of Jesus' time
Time	Jesus' time
Cast	PETER — a disciple of Jesus
	RUTH — his wife.

PETER: (*ARRIVING HOME*) Hi, honey. I'm home.

RUTH: (*OFF STAGE*) Is that you, honey?

PETER: Of course, it's me. I'm home.

RUTH: Just put the fish on the fire, will you? I'll be in in a minute.

PETER: (*TO HIMSELF*) I don't have any fish.

RUTH: What's that, dear?

PETER: Nothing, dear.

RUTH: (*ENTERS*) Did you have a nice weekend, dear? (*SHE GIVES HIM A HUG AND KISS*) Oh, you better change that old cloak. You've gotten it all wet. Dear, you didn't put the fish on the fire.

PETER: There aren't any fish.

RUTH: You're a fisherman. What do you mean, there aren't any fish?

PETER: We didn't go fishing.

RUTH: You're a fisherman. You look like a fisherman. You certainly smell like a fisherman. Didn't you catch any fish again?

PETER: We didn't go fishing.

RUTH: You didn't go fishing? You went out with the guys.

PETER: On another mission.

RUTH: What was it this time?

PETER: Well, Jesus performed some exciting miracles.

RUTH: He's doing that a lot, isn't He?

PETER: He sure is.

RUTH: What is it this time? More healing I suppose.

PETER: He did a little of that, of course — those who wanted to be healed. No, this time He concentrated on feeding 5000.

RUTH: What's that? Five thousand people? He fed 5000 people?

PETER: Actually there were more than that. That's just all the men we could get counted.

RUTH: He fed that many? How did He do that?

PETER: Well, it was great. There was this kid there with a couple of fish and some bread and Jesus just made it become more somehow.

RUTH: That's a lot of fish and bread.

PETER: And we had twelve basketfuls left over.

RUTH: Are you telling me you had that much left over and you didn't even bring home a fish?

PETER: That's about it.

RUTH: I bet Matthew took home a fish to his wife.

PETER: No, he didn't.

RUTH: He didn't?

PETER: No, he didn't. No one did.

RUTH: Well, what happened to the leftovers?

PETER: It's a long story.

RUTH: I'm all ears.

PETER: Yeah, well, we were just preparing to come home and Jesus made us get in the boat and leave without Him.

RUTH: How was He getting home?

PETER: I'm getting to that. So, there we were rowing and one of those nasty little storms blows up, you know, and we were getting the worst of it.

RUTH: And you had the twelve basketfuls of food?

PETER: Don't rush me. Yes, the baskets were in the bottom of the boat but the waves got so bad the bread was getting all soaked and then all the food was washed overboard anyway.

RUTH: No wonder you're all wet.

PETER: There's more.

RUTH: Okay, go on.

PETER: All right. Well, there we were getting soaked and being driven farther from the shore and guess what we saw?

RUTH: I don't know. What?

PETER: Jesus.

RUTH: Jesus?

PETER: Jesus. Right. There He was, walking on the water.

RUTH: Wait a minute. Wait just a little minute. Peter, I don't mind you telling these tales of healings. I saw Mother healed, but don't you think walking on the water is a bit too much to be believed?

PETER: I'm not kidding. He was walking on the water. Actually walking on the water.

RUTH: What will He think of next?

PETER: A lot of the guys thought He was a ghost.

RUTH: A ghost! I guess they would think that. Imagine, walking on the water. Why would He do that?

PETER: Maybe because it was the quickest way to get to us. I don't know. It doesn't matter. The fact was He was walking on the water.

RUTH: I don't know. Walking on water. I just don't know. Next He'll have you doing crazy stunts like that. Well, what happened next?

PETER: (*PAUSE*) Well, I, ah ... (*IN A SMALL VOICE*) I walked on the water, too.

RUTH: What?

PETER: Now, don't get excited. I just had to try it too.

RUTH: Walking on water?

PETER: Yes. I did it, too.

RUTH: You?

PETER: I did. I just said, "Lord, if that's really you, tell me to come to you and I will."

RUTH: And He did?

PETER: Right. He did and then I walked on the water, too.

RUTH: How far?

PETER: What?

RUTH: I said, how far? How far did you walk on the water?

PETER: (*IN A SMALL VOICE*) About ten feet.

RUTH: Ten feet? That's it?

PETER: Well, how far have you walked on the water?

RUTH: That's not the point, is it? The point is all this hullabaloo and you didn't even bring home any fish for dinner.

PETER: That's not the point.

RUTH: Well, what is the point?

PETER: I'm going to tell you the point. The point is I walked on the water.

RUTH: Ten feet.

PETER: Well, I did it anyway. And I know I did it for sure.

RUTH: Wait a minute. What happened after ten feet? Did you stub your toe on a wave?

PETER: (*IN A SMALL VOICE*) I got scared.

RUTH: (*SHOWING CONCERN*) You got scared?

PETER: And then I began to sink. But Jesus reached out His hand and saved me.

RUTH: So that's how you got all wet.

PETER: Yeah.

RUTH: Well, here, let me help you out of that cloak. It's water logged. Aren't you my water walker.

PETER: I sure am.

RUTH: Well, would you look at this! (*PULLING A FISH OUT OF HIS CLOAK*)

PETER: I guess I am a fisherman after all.

Demonized

Theme
    Jesus has total control over the powers of darkness.

Summary
    A mother talks to a psychiatrist about her demonized daughter and how she was delivered. The psychiatrist won't accept the healing.

Playing Time	3 minutes
Setting	The office of Dr. Willis
Props	A file folder, a new book
Costumes	Contemporary
Time	The present
Cast	DR. WILLIS — a psychiatrist
	MRS. KING
	DEBBIE — her daughter

DR. WILLIS: (*ENTERS WITH MRS. KING*) Sit down, please. Mrs. King, your daughter ...

MRS. KING: I can't sit. Debbie ...

DR. WILLIS: As I was about to say, Mrs. King, your daughter has been responding to my treatment very well.

MRS. KING: No, she hasn't, Dr. Willis. That's why I'm here.

DR. WILLIS: These things take time. Remember, I told you that when we began these treatments.

MRS. KING: I remember you said my daughter was schizophrenic.

DR. WILLIS: (*GLANCING AT FOLDER*) A paranoid type with delusional features.

MRS. KING: I remember.

DR. WILLIS: Debbie's schizophrenia is probably a result of a chemical imbalance and poor brain circuitry.

MRS. KING: Not in her case. I know that's what you thought in the beginning, but as it turned out it was a spiritual problem, not a physical one. She was demonized.

DR. WILLIS: Mrs. King, I think we talked about this. There are no such things as demons, and therefore there is no such condition as being demonized. Your daughter is not demonized. She has schizophrenia.

MRS. KING: She was demonized, Doctor.

DR. WILLIS: Mrs. King, I think it would be better if you didn't speak about such things. These are your own fantasies and cannot but do harm to the child.

MRS. KING: But, Dr. Willis, I know that these problems began when Debbie became involved in the New Age teachings.

DR. WILLIS: The New Age movement has done a lot of good.

MRS. KING: Hardly. It was New Age teaching about channeling that got Debbie into trouble. She had a spirit guide. That's how she got demonized. The spirit guide that seemed so good to her at first was a demon.

DR. WILLIS: Mrs. King, it's difficult to communicate with you when you keep insisting that your daughter is demonized.

MRS. KING: Dr. Willis, it's just as difficult for me to communicate with you as it is for you to communicate with me when you don't acknowledge a basic truth.

DR. WILLIS: Mrs. King, you are the one who discontinued the treatments. We have seen remarkable improvement sometimes in less than a year. I'm a busy man. I insist that you bring Debbie in to see me and continue treatments and stop this nonsense about demons and being demonized.

MRS. KING: You never understood the causes of my daughter's problems and therefore you could never have helped her.

DR. WILLIS: Mrs. King, I'm sure that we can work out our little differences.

MRS. KING: I don't see them as little differences. There is a spiritual world, Dr. Willis, whether you acknowledge it or not.

DR. WILLIS: My experience has taught me no such thing.

MRS. KING: Debbie was subtly educated in the New Age teachings.

DR. WILLIS: You need to bring Debbie back to me.

MRS. KING: Oh, no, Dr. Willis. Debbie doesn't need you, now. She is healed. We had a deliverance and Jesus healed her.

DR. WILLIS: Preposterous!

MRS. KING: Only the power of God can save a person who is demonized and that's why Debbie is whole again.

DR. WILLIS: I think you'd be wise, Mrs. King, to bring Debbie in to see me and to continue my treatments.

MRS. KING: She's in the waiting room. You can see that she's well.

DR. WILLIS: All right, we'll see.

MRS. KING: Debbie, honey, would you come in and see Dr. Willis.

DEBBIE: *(ENTERS)* Hello, Dr. Willis. Did Mother tell you about my deliverance?

DR. WILLIS: Er, yes. Yes, she did. Ah, Debbie, how do you feel?

DEBBIE: I feel just fine. Great, in fact. I've been set free, Doctor. I'm me again.

DR. WILLIS: Set free? Free from what?

DEBBIE: All the lies I believed — and hurting myself. I'm free.

DR. WILLIS: Yes, uh, thank you, Debbie. May I talk to your mother alone?

DEBBIE: Sure, doctor. Good-bye. (*SHE EXITS*)

MRS. KING: Well, Doctor, what do you think? You can see she is well now.

DR. WILLIS: Hmmm. This certainly is an unusual development. I'd like to continue my treatment to make sure she's stabilized.

MRS. KING: She's gone back to school and is doing fine. She knows now to test everything against the Word of God and she knows how important it is to have Christian friends.

DR. WILLIS: Mrs. King, I believe you are both deluded. To think that the organized church can be an instrument in healing is ridiculous.

MRS. KING: Doctor, Debbie and I came in today to share with you the spiritual root of her problem. There are many Christian psychiatrists today that would agree with me. I brought this book. I hope you will read it. (*HANDS HIM THE BOOK*)

DR. WILLIS: Your daughter needs professional help. What I should do is to notify the proper authorities concerning this.

MRS. KING: Good bye, Doctor. (*SHE EXITS*)

Who Is God?

Theme

There are many false gods. Finding God isn't easy but it is worth the search.

Summary

Two people are talking about God and each gives several views. "God" is watching from above. Jesus enters and exposes "God" as a fraud and offers the two a real relationship with God.

Playing Time	6 minutes
Setting	A neutral acting space
Props	Ladder, policeman's cap, glasses, ruler, Santa Claus cap and beard, gray beard, menu, stuffed lamb, halo, crutch, lemon, box, and magnifying glass
Costumes	Contemporary
Time	The present
Cast	"GOD" — a false god
	PLAYER 1
	PLAYER 2
	JESUS

(*GOD ENTERS CARRYING A LADDER, PLACES IT CENTER STAGE, CLIMBS TO THE TOP AND SITS*)

PLAYER 1: (*ENTERS WITH PLAYER 2*) Oh, wow, man, I just had another flat tire and my spare was flat, too.

PLAYER 2: Boy, doesn't that make you mad?

PLAYER 1: It sure does. Where was God all that time?

PLAYER 2: Yeah, I know what you mean. God is like a police-man. (*GOD PUTS ON POLICEMAN'S CAP*) Ya know what I mean? Never around when you need him, but boy, run a red light and he's right there!

PLAYER 1: I know what you mean.

PLAYER 2: God is always ready to condemn me when I make a mistake.

PLAYER 1: Like my fourth grade teacher. (*GOD TAKES POLICEMAN'S CAP OFF AND PUTS GLASSES ON END OF NOSE AND SLAPS RULER AGAINST HIS HAND*) I remember she would spank your hands with a ruler when you did something wrong.

PLAYER 2: I had a teacher like that but she would never waste an opportunity like that by merely spanking your hand.

PLAYER 1: Yeah, right. God knows where it hurts, too.

PLAYER 2: You know, I used to have a pretty good idea of who God is. I used to think He was kinda like a Santa Claus, you know. (*GOD TAKES OFF GLASSES AND PUTS ON SANTA CAP AND BEARD*) "He knows when you are sleeping, he knows when you're awake, he knows if you've been bad or good, so be good for good-ness sake."

PLAYER 1: "Oh, you better watch out, you better not cry, better not pout, I'm telling you why, God is gonna get you in the end."

PLAYER 2: Right. Then when I was a kid I thought of God as the grandfather in the sky who would love me no matter what and give me candy when I fell and hurt my knee. (*GOD TAKES OFF SANTA COSTUME AND PUTS ON GRAY BEARD*)

PLAYER 1: I always thought of God as old fashioned. I figured if He was around to create the world He was too old to relate to me.

PLAYER 2: Yeah, I'll admit that God did a lot for the people in the Bible, but how can He relate to the complex society that we live in today?

PLAYER 1: Well, that's the point, isn't it?

PLAYER 2: Exactly. That is the point. God is kinda out to lunch as far as doing anything about the difficulties in the world today. (*GOD TAKES OF BEARD AND BEGINS TO READ MENU*)

PLAYER 1: Do you know what used to get me? The pictures of Jesus holding that little lamb. (*GOD PUTS AWAY MENU AND PICKS UP STUFFED LAMB*) I mean, what has that got to do with me? I'm not a sheep.

PLAYER 2: Not a ba-a-ad point. Why couldn't the little lamb walk by itself? All the little lambs I've seen could walk by themselves.

PLAYER 1: Right you are. And all those old paintings picture Jesus as this weak, skinny guy in His night shirt with a kind of a dopey grin on His face. Who can relate to a guy like that?

PLAYER 2: "Gentle Jesus, meek and mild, look upon a little child." Even as a kid I couldn't relate to a God like that. When I was a kid I was thinking of baseball in the summer and the opposite sex all the time. The God I saw in those paintings never thought about anything except the Ten Commandments and how He hadn't broken any of them. (*GOD PUTS LAMB AWAY AND PUTS ON HALO*)

PLAYER 1: God is perfect, right?

PLAYER 2: Right.

PLAYER 1: Right. That's a little difficult to understand.

PLAYER 2: The Bible does say that. Be perfect as God is perfect.

PLAYER 1: I've tried that.

PLAYER 2: How long did it last?

PLAYER 1: About ten minutes. Then I realized I was proud because I was so perfect and pride is a sin so I wasn't perfect after all. I can't relate to a perfect God. Perfect? Not me. I can't even get the part in my hair straight.

PLAYER 2: Tell me something, do you think of Christianity as an escape?

PLAYER 1: I know what you're thinking. You think that people who become Christians are running away from the real world.

PLAYER 2: That's it. Therefore God is a God of escape.

PLAYER 1: And Christians need a crutch. I just can't relate to that either. (*GOD PUTS HALO AWAY AND TAKES OUT CRUTCH*)

PLAYER 2: Neither can I.

PLAYER 1: You know what turns me off to Christianity? It's Christians.

PLAYER 2: You're not going to say that they're hypocrites.

PLAYER 1: No, I wasn't, but some are. No, I was thinking that they are so boring.

PLAYER 2: Yeah, they are, aren't they. So prim and proper. Who could get interested in a God that wanted His people to be like that?

PLAYER 1: Most Christians look like they've been sucking on a lemon. (*GOD PUTS AWAY CRUTCH AND SUCKS ON A LEMON*)

PLAYER 2: They have their own god, don't they?

PLAYER 1: What are you talking about?

PLAYER 2: They put God in their own little box. (*GOD PUTS LEMON AWAY AND PUTS A BOX OVER HIS HEAD*)

PLAYER 1: Who'd want a God like that?

PLAYER 2: We are being quite theological today, aren't we?

PLAYER 1: Yes, we are. And we're doing it quite well.

PLAYER 2: Tiresome, isn't it?

PLAYER 1: Yes, it is.

PLAYER 2: When it comes right down to it, isn't God just a projection of ourselves and our society?

PLAYER 1: Now you are getting deep.

PLAYER 2: Here's what I mean: Don't people see the attributes of God that are really their own attributes but just magnified? (*GOD PUTS BOX AWAY AND BRINGS OUT MAGNIFYING GLASS*)

PLAYER 1: I see what you mean. A person with a strict upbringing would think God is all laws and rules and not a loving God.

PLAYER 2: That's it. And a person who is morally lax would worship a God who is a very forgiving God.

PLAYER 1: Do you know what? I don't think I can relate to God.

PLAYER 2: Me neither. Not at all.

PLAYER 1: It is fun relating my views to you though.

PLAYER 2: Yes, it is fun. We must do it again sometime.

PLAYER 1: Yes, we must.

PLAYER 2: I wonder what God would say if He were here.

PLAYER 1: He'd probably say, "I wonder why I'm standing here in my nightshirt with this dopey grin on my face?"

PLAYER 2: And why am I carrying this lamb?

GOD: Are you two enjoying yourself?

PLAYER 1: Yes, we are.

PLAYER 2: Who are you?

PLAYER 1: And what are you doing up there?

GOD: I'm God. And you should not be questioning who I am. You should be worshiping me.

PLAYER 1: Forgive us, God.

PLAYER 2: Yes, we didn't know.

GOD: Well, now that you know, get on with it. Worship me.

PLAYER 1: All right.

PLAYER 2: Sure, right away. (*THEY BEGIN TO WORSHIP*)

JESUS: (*ENTERS, DRESSED CASUALLY*) What's going on?

PLAYER 1: We're just worshiping God.

JESUS: Nonsense!

PLAYER 2: Nonsense?

PLAYER 1: But, you can't talk like that. That's God.

JESUS: I'm God.

PLAYER 2: You?

JESUS: Yes, I'm Jesus.

PLAYER 2: Then who is that up there?

GOD: I'm God.

JESUS: No, you're not. Come down from there. (*GOD DESCENDS*)

PLAYER 1: This is kinda confusing.

JESUS: Get your stuff and get out of here.

GOD: But, I'm God.

JESUS: No, you're not. You're a false god. All the false gods they were talking about.

GOD: But ...

JESUS: Out! (*GOD EXITS TAKING LADDER AND PROPS*)

PLAYER 1: Do you mean all those things we were saying about God were untrue?

JESUS: You both have a pretty narrow view of me.

PLAYER 2: How do we find out about who you really are?

JESUS: Just spend time with me.

PLAYER 1: That's too easy.

JESUS: Not so easy, but worthwhile. Want to try?

PLAYER 2: Yeah.

PLAYER 1: You bet. (*THEY ALL BEGIN TO EXIT*)

JESUS: Nightshirt and dopey grin, indeed.

PLAYER 1: Let me explain ...

The One Chosen

Theme

There are those who would stop us from doing God's best and want us to do what is only good. They are stumbling blocks to us. Jesus is always our model for life and death.

Summary

In a time in the future, when the government is exterminating children who are inferior and sterilizing parents who bear them, two people struggle whether to put their lives in danger to save others.

Playing Time	4 minutes
Setting	The home of Itzak and Morah
Props	A knapsack
Costumes	Peasant
Time	The future
Cast	ITZAK
	MORAH — his wife

MORAH: (*ENTERS WITH ITZAK. THEY EMBRACE*) Stay with me.

ITZAK: I can't.

MORAH: You can't go back.

ITZAK: I must. You know I must.

MORAH: I know I prayed and God brought you back to me.

ITZAK: I prayed, too. I prayed that God would allow me to come back to you. And He did, but ...

MORAH: No. Don't say it. Stay here with me. I love you.

ITZAK: I must go. If the passports are not delivered, the Lord knows how many children will be trapped in the city.

MORAH: What about our own children if you are caught? Have you thought about them?

ITZAK: Of course I have. I've agonized about them. I know the chance I'm taking and the peril I'm putting you and the children in. This is something I have to do. You know that. We both agreed this is something we could do for the abandoned ones.

MORAH: They're lost anyway. The government will find them and exterminate them. Sooner or later they will find them.

ITZAK: Not if we can smuggle the passports in to them and get them out of the country.

MORAH: You said the last time you left that that was all the runs you would make. You said that.

ITZAK: I know. I know what I said. But they found more children. They were hiding in the sewers. We've got to get them out before the government finds them.

MORAH: What if you don't come back this time? I think of that all the time. What if they stop you and search you? You know what they'll do to you.

ITZAK: Yes, I know.

MORAH: Do you love me?

ITZAK: You know I do.

MORAH: Then don't go this time. Let someone else do it. Let Runare do it. He's not married.

ITZAK: Runare didn't return.

MORAH: You see. You see! It's too dangerous. You can't go. Stay here with us. Please, Itzak. Please!

ITZAK: Please, Morah, don't do this.

MORAH: Please, listen to me. Just listen to me. We can get out of the country ourselves. We can get away. I can't stand living in this oppressive place any longer. We have to get out of the country. We could do that. We could.

ITZAK: Morah, please don't.

MORAH: Just listen. You could get us passports. You know you could. We could slip out of the country. It would be easy. You've done your bit for humanity.

ITZAK: The job isn't done yet. I have to finish the job. Now, Morah, we decided this is something we would do.

MORAH: But I didn't know it would be so difficult. I can't give you up. I can't.

ITZAK: You're not giving me up. I'll be back.

MORAH: You don't know that.

ITZAK: I'll be back.

MORAH: I won't let you go.

ITZAK: Morah, you can't stop me. You mustn't try. Morah, didn't we both pray about this?

MORAH: Yes,

ITZAK: And we both thought the Lord wanted me to do this.

MORAH: I know.

ITZAK: Do you still feel the Lord wants those children saved?

MORAH: Of course I do.

ITZAK: There's no one else to do it. I'm their only way out.

MORAH: I'm scared, Itzak. I need you here with me.

ITZAK: Morah, don't be a hindrance to me.

MORAH: A hindrance? But I love you.

ITZAK: If you try to stop me, you're going against what we thought to be God's will.

MORAH: I know. I'm torn.

ITZAK: I am too. But we must be strong. I need you to be strong. You have to stay here and protect our children. I must go and try to save the others. You won't be with me but we are working together.

MORAH: No. We won't be together. We'll be apart.

ITZAK: We'll never be apart if we are sure of the same mind on what we are to do. We can only trust God and do what seems right to us.

MORAH: You are right. You speak truth but it hurts so much.

ITZAK: Yes. Now, say good-bye. The sooner I leave the quicker I'll return. (*THEY EMBRACE. HE EXITS*)

MORAH: Good-bye, my husband, my love.

My Brother's Keeper

Theme

We are not only responsible for ourselves in the Kingdom of God, but for others as well.

Summary

Thomas and Matthew are trying to decide who will confront Judas about his sinful ways.

Playing Time	3 minutes
Setting	The Holy Land
Props	None
Costumes	Disciples of Jesus
Time	The time of Jesus
Cast	MATTHEW
	THOMAS

MATTHEW: (*ENTERS WITH THOMAS*) Jesus told us to do it.

THOMAS: I know, but I just can't do it, Matthew.

MATTHEW: It has to be done. Look, Thomas, I've been to see him once.

THOMAS: You've been to him already? I thought we were going together.

MATTHEW: That's not what the Master told us to do. I'm supposed to go to him and confront him with his sin, and he's supposed to confess and repent and ...

271

THOMAS: Yes, of course. I remember now. Well, what happened? What did he say?

MATTHEW: I confronted him about the shortage and he said he didn't do it. It was that simple.

THOMAS: He said he didn't do it. Well, what would you expect him to say, "Sure, I stole all the money from the offerings"?

MATTHEW: Jesus said that's the way it's supposed to work.

THOMAS: Well, you just learned something. It doesn't always work out like the Master says.

MATTHEW: It would be nicer if it would.

THOMAS: "Nicer" is not reality, Matthew. We're dealing with sin here, not "nicer."

MATTHEW: I guess so. Well, what do we do?

THOMAS: You know what we do. We both go to him and we take along another brother, maybe Simon. Simon will stare him down and then he'll confess and then he'll repent and we'll forgive him and we'll all be all right again.

MATTHEW: Like Jesus said, "Then we have won our brother."

THOMAS: That's right.

MATTHEW: But you don't want to go and confront him.

THOMAS: I don't like to confront anybody But it has to be done. For our sake and for his. I can see how it might work. If he is caught in this sin and confesses and repents, it might stop him from doing something worse.

MATTHEW: Well, I don't want to confront him again. But we have to.

THOMAS: That's why we're going to take Simon along. Simon loves to confront anybody at any time.

MATTHEW: Right. We take Simon.

THOMAS: We might as well go do it now. (*THEY BEGIN TO EXIT*) What's going to happen to him?

MATTHEW: What do you mean?

THOMAS: I mean, if he doesn't repent, what's going to happen to him?

MATTHEW: I don't really know. I don't understand him.

THOMAS: Neither do I. Judas is different.

The King Forgives Sometimes

Theme
Forgive others as God through Jesus has forgiven you.

Summary
In this modern parable a man owes the King (Elvis) a lot of money and Elvis forgives him until he finds out the man is unforgiving to another who owes him money.

Playing Time	3 minutes
Setting	Graceland
Props	None
Costumes	Elvis — white sequins with cape
	Others — casual
Time	When Elvis was King
Cast	ELVIS
	WILLARD — a person who works for Elvis
	SAM — another such person

SAM: (*ENTERS WITH WILLARD*) Hey, Willard, did you see the King yet?

WILLARD: No, and I don't want to.

SAM: How come?

WILLARD: I owe him a little money.

SAM: Aw, that's no problem. The King is very generous. A lot of times he just considers it a gift and lets it go at that. You never have to pay it back.

WILLARD: I'm a little worried about it.

SAM: How much do you owe him?

WILLARD: Ten million.

SAM: Wow! Are you serious?

WILLARD: Serious as a broken leg.

SAM: Ten million!

WILLARD: What do you think he'll do to me?

SAM: Ten million is a lot for the King to forgive.

WILLARD: Don't I know it.

SAM: Here comes the King.

ELVIS: (*ENTERS*) Thank you very much, ladies and gentlemen. (*SINGING*) "You Saw Me Crying In The Chapel." (*SPEAKING*) Hello, Willard, you here to pay me my money?

WILLARD: No, Sir, King, Sir.

ELVIS: (*SINGING*) "You Ain't Nothin' But A Hound Dog."

WILLARD: Er, that's right, Mr. King, Sir. Just give me a chance to pay it back.

ELVIS: (*SINGING*) "I Got Stung." (*SPEAKING*) Ten million dollars, Willard. (*SINGING*) " It's Now Or Never."

WILLARD: I can't pay you now.

ELVIS: (*SPEAKING*) Willard, you didn't. (*SINGING*) "Return To Sender." (*SPEAKING*) All right, Willard, I'll get my money one way or another. I'm going to have all your property sold including having your wife and children and yourself auctioned off. (*SINGING*) "Surrender."

WILLARD: Oh, King, be patient with me and I will pay it all.

ELVIS: (*SINGING*) "Too Much." (*SPEAKING*) You can't pay that back. I'll tell you what. You're forgiven. You don't have to pay me back. Forget it.

WILLARD: Thank you. Thank you. (*HUGS ELVIS*)

ELVIS: (*EXITS, SINGING*) "A Fool Such As I."

SAM: (*ENTERS*) Willard, what happened?

WILLARD: Never mind. You owe me two thousand dollars. Where is it?

SAM: Have a heart, Willard. I can't pay. Can you wait? I'll pay you back.

WILLARD: Forget it. You're going to jail until you can come up with the money.

SAM: (*EXITS*) Oh, no.

ELVIS: (*ENTERS*) What's going on, Willard? I just saw Sam and he said you were going to have him arrested and thrown in jail for a debt of two thousand dollars. I thought you learned. (*SINGING*) "Don't Be Cruel."

WILLARD: But I thought ...

ELVIS: Willard, you look (*SINGING*) "All Shook Up."

WILLARD: I'm sorry.

ELVIS: (*SINGING*) "You're The Devil In Disguise." (*SPEAK-ING*) That's it. I'm angry. I forgave your tremendous debt (*SING-ING*) "Just For You" just because you asked me to and you won't forgive another? You're going to be doing the (*SINGING*) "Jail House Rock."

WILLARD: (*EXITS*) Oh, no.

ELVIS: (*SINGING*) "Don't Cry, Daddy." (*SPEAKING*) Listen, ladies and gentlemen, (*SINGING*) "Don't, I Beg You" (*SPEAKING*) do the same as he did. God's going to get tough with you if you don't forgive. Do it and then you'll have (*SING-ING*) "Peace In The Valley." (*EXITS, SPEAKING*) Thank you very much, ladies and gentlemen.

Payday

Theme

God's generosity to all.

Summary

Two workers get their pay. One worked a full eight hours, the other only one hour. The owner paid them both a full day's wage. The worker who worked all day is upset with the owner and wants to take it to court.

Playing Time	4 minutes
Setting	A factory
Props	Pay receipts
Costumes	Marge, Susan — work clothes
	Mr. Jones — suit
Time	The present
Cast	JONES — the owner of a small industrial plant
	MARGE — a worker
	SUSAN — a worker

JONES: (*ENTERS WITH MARGE*) Here, let me sign that receipt from your agency.

MARGE: Hey, Mr. Jones, is there any chance for permanent work here?

JONES: There might be for you. You're a good worker. But you have to put your application in.

MARGE: Okay, I'll do that.

JONES: (*HANDING MARGE THE RECEIPT*) I'll keep you in mind for work tomorrow morning.

MARGE: Great. Thanks. (*EXITS*)

JONES: Okay, who's next?

SUSAN: I am. Here's my card.

JONES: Oh, yes, I see you only worked an hour today.

SUSAN: The agency called me late, but I came right over as soon as I could get here.

JONES: Did you like the work?

SUSAN: I liked it well enough.

JONES: (*HANDING RECEIPT BACK TO HER*) I'll keep you in mind for tomorrow.

SUSAN: Thanks. (*JONES EXITS*)

MARGE: (*ENTERS*) Hey, how you doing?

SUSAN: All right.

MARGE: Wanna do something after work?

SUSAN: I have to get home.

MARGE: You don't have time?

SUSAN: No.

MARGE: Well, how'd you like the work?

SUSAN: It's work. It's okay.

MARGE: (*LOOKING AT HER RECEIPT*) Pretty good pay.

SUSAN: Yeah. (*LOOKING AT HER RECEIPT*) What in the world?

MARGE: What's wrong?

SUSAN: Wrong? Nothing's wrong. Just with the owner's math, maybe.

MARGE: What is it? I'd sure tell him if I got gypped on my pay.

SUSAN: He didn't gyp me. He paid me for eight hours.

MARGE: Well?

SUSAN: But, I only worked one hour.

MARGE: What the ... (*GRABBING SUSAN'S RECEIPT*) Let me see that.

SUSAN: What do you think?

MARGE: Why, that ... who does he think he is? I'm going to straighten this out. (*CROSSING TOWARD JONES*) You got paid as much as I did. And I put in a full day's work. (*JONES ENTERS*) Hey, what is this?

JONES: What's the problem?

MARGE: You paid her as much as you paid me.

JONES: And how does that concern you?

MARGE: She worked an hour and I worked all day.

JONES: I paid you fairly for the work you did.

MARGE: And why did you pay her a full day's wage?

JONES: Because I wanted to. I own this shop.

MARGE: We'll see about this. My brother-in-law was telling me about someone who was discriminated against and he went to the ACLU and they sued the guy.

JONES: You feel you were discriminated against here, right?

MARGE: Right. I worked all day. She worked one hour.

SUSAN: I worked hard.

MARGE: One hour.

SUSAN: I didn't know he was going to pay me for eight hours. I was going to ask him about it but you ripped the slip out of my hand before I could.

MARGE: *(TO JONES)* You are going to answer to my lawyer.

JONES: I will do that when and if it is necessary.

SUSAN: Are you going to correct my receipt?

JONES: No, I'm not.

SUSAN: Why did you pay me for eight hours?

JONES: Do you have a family?

SUSAN: Yes, three children.

JONES: Then you need the money.

MARGE: I need the money for my family, too.

JONES: Why should my generosity be a reason for you to accuse me of wrongdoing? Go home to your family.

MARGE: You haven't heard the last of this.

SUSAN: (*TO JONES*) Thank you.

JONES: You're welcome. (*HE EXITS*)

SUSAN: It looks like to me you can't understand a good deed when you see one because you've probably never done one.

MARGE: You call that a good deed? I call it robbery and he hasn't heard the last of me. (*SHE EXITS*)

SUSAN: I wonder who the owner will call for work tomorrow?

Knock, Knock!

Theme
What if the people in the Kingdom of God are not like us? Will we welcome them, help them, love them?

Summary
A couple are surprised to have guests, an IRS man and a prostitute, who are seeking information about the Kingdom of God. The couple are unwilling to help them and finally kick them out of their home.

Playing Time	3 minutes
Setting	A normal Christian home
Props	A cellular phone
Costumes	Contemporary, casual appropriate for characters
Time	The present
Cast	MITCH — a Christian businessman
	VERNA — his wife
	WINNY — an IRS man
	SUGAR — a prostitute

MITCH: (*ENTERS. ON THE PHONE*) Yes, take care of the Williams account.

VERNA: (*ENTERS ALONG WITH WINNY AND SUGAR*) Honey, we have some guests.

WINNY: Hello.

MITCH: Listen, I'll call you back. (*HANGS UP PHONE*) Yes?

VERNA: Make yourself at home.

SUGAR: Thanks.

WINNY: Hi, we're here about the Kingdom of God.

MITCH: Sorry. I'm not interested.

WINNY: You are part of it, aren't you?

MITCH: The Kingdom of God? Of course. I belong to the Lord.

WINNY: Well, we want to know all about it.

MITCH: Are you selling magazines?

WINNY: No.

MITCH: Well, I'm not interested anyway.

WINNY: We just want to find out about the Kingdom of God.

MITCH: I'm really busy.

WINNY: Could you just share with us about God?

VERNA: How wonderful. Of course we will, won't we, dear.

MITCH: Who are you?

WINNY: My name is Winfield Stratton. I work for the IRS and this is ...

MITCH: The IRS! I get it. You want to audit my return.

WINNY: Not at all. I just want to know about the Kingdom of God.

284

MITCH: I think that's pretty tricky, slipping in here, telling me you're interested in finding out about God.

WINNY: We do want to find out about God. We heard that you knew the Lord and therefore we thought that you might help us.

MITCH: Well, you thought wrong.

VERNA: Dear, maybe we could be of some help to these fine people.

MITCH: You just stay out of this. Let me handle it.

VERNA: (*TO SUGAR*) Hello, my dear. It's so nice to have you in my home. I'm sure my husband and I can answer all your questions about the Kingdom of God.

SUGAR: Thanks.

WINNY: Now we're getting somewhere. Could you tell us how to become a part of God's Kingdom?

VERNA: Of course we'll help, won't we, dear.

MITCH: No! I thought I made it clear. You're not welcome here.

WINNY: I just thought ...

MITCH: No. No more talk. Just leave. Leave my house.

VERNA: Must you be so harsh? All they want is to hear about the Kingdom of God. Surely we, as Christians ...

MITCH: I told you to keep out of it. I don't want any snooping IRS man here. He just wants to audit me.

VERNA: I don't think so, dear.

WINNY: I assure you, Sir, I didn't come to audit your tax return.

MITCH: That's what you say.

VERNA: Dear, isn't it our Christian duty to help those who want to learn about the Kingdom of God? I think it is.

WINNY: Thank you, Ma'am.

MITCH: You two just get out of here, now! (*HE SHOVES WINNY AND SUGAR*)

VERNA: Here, now, there's no need to get violent.

MITCH: Just get them out of here.

VERNA: (*WITH HER ARM AROUND SUGAR*) Are you all right? I hope he didn't hurt you. What's your name, dear?

SUGAR: Sugar.

VERNA: Sugar. That's an interesting name — Sugar.

SUGAR: It's not my real name.

VERNA: Well, my dear, it's a really pretty name. What is it you do, dear?

SUGAR: I'm a prostitute.

VERNA: What?

SUGAR: A prostitute, you know, I ...

VERNA: Are you serious?

SUGAR: Yes, I'm afraid so.

VERNA: Well, you better get out of here.

WINNY: What about the Kingdom of God?

VERNA: Forget it! Get out of here! (*WINNY AND SUGAR EXIT*) The nerve. Imagine.

MITCH: The Kingdom of God was not made for the likes of those scum.

The Wicked Pie Bakers

Theme

Is the church a place where the Christian community gathers to celebrate or a place where the law is administered? Are we open or closed to new ideas? A parable.

Summary

The choir is having a bake sale and the discussion is whether that is a good or bad thing to have in church.

A light-hearted, fast-paced discussion about the Pharisees and the tax gatherers and how we can kill the Spirit of Jesus in each other by being too judgmental.

Playing Time	3 minutes
Setting	Your church
Props	None
Costumes	Appropriate for church
Time	The present
Cast	SANDY — announcement maker
	DON — he's hungry
	JO — reasonable.
	VOICE — actually attached to a person
	SAM — A serious one

SANDY: (*ENTERS. SPEAKS INTO MICROPHONE*) The choir is having a bake sale to raise money for their trip to Ireland next year, so everyone go and buy the goodies that will be waiting for you and your family. The table will be set up in the fellowship hall.

DON: (*FROM WAY IN THE BACK*) What's that? We can't hear back here.

SANDY: Right after church in the red room.

DON: What's right after church?

JO: (*IN THE CONGREGATION, NEAR DON*) A bake sale.

DON: Oh, I heard that, all right. A bake sale!

SANDY: And we're praying that the Lord will bless our evangelism.

VOICE: (*FROM THE CONGREGATION*) Hallelujah!

SANDY: Right. Praise the Lord.

SAM: (*STANDS IN CONGREGATION*) I don't believe a bake sale in the church glorifies God and His work.

JO: (*STANDING*) Oh, I don't know. We sell stuff in the book store and that glorifies God, doesn't it?

SAM: What about the money changers in the Temple?

DON: (*STANDING*) If you're worried about the money changers we won't let them in this church. I'll volunteer to stand at the door Sunday and stop them. "Sir, are you a money changer? I'm sorry, you're not allowed in here. Would you mind going to the Bath Community Church, please. They might need some money changed over there."

SAM: Wise guy. This is serious. Do you think we ought to have bake sales in the church?

DON: Well, no, I don't.

SAM: There, you see.

DON: But having them in the fellowship hall is fine with me.

JO: You can't put God in a box.

DON: No, but you can put cookies in a box. I know, a box cake. I'll even buy a box cake.

SAM: "You can't put God in a box." What's that, the slogan for the week? There have to be some rules in churches, don't you think? Otherwise people will just do whatever they want. Like Israel back in the times of the judges.

JO: Sometimes I wonder if it was good for you to take that Bible study course.

SAM: Everyone who joins the church should be required to take the same course I did.

DON: Lord, help us.

SAM: What's that supposed to mean?

DON: "Lord help us"? It means we need help so why not pray. You see, prayer is an open line to God which we can use to ask for things, petition God, or we can just say praise the Lord.

VOICE: Hallelujah!

SAM: What we need is the sword of the Lord to reap some judgment around here.

JO: And you'd be the sword, eh?

SAM: No, Jesus is the sword of judgment. To clean out the church — to set us on the straight and narrow path again. If everyone would give their tithe as it states clearly in the scriptures we wouldn't have to have bake sales to raise money.

JO: Or book stores.

SAM: Well, maybe so. I think we have to do some repenting ...

VOICE: Praise God!

SAM: Yes, we have to do some repenting about the attitudes we have about how to run a church. Bake sales — really!

DON: I can't wait to buy some of Jan's fudge.

SAM: We can't be running our church like General Motors.

DON: How about a foreign import — Danish pastry.

SAM: I see I can't talk to you.

JO: You can talk, but will you listen?

SAM: I get so fed up with people not doing right around here. I told Pam just the other day that she had to get her act together or the Lord was going to punish her.

DON: Remember those chocolate chip cookies Nancy baked for the Christmas party last year?

JO: Why don't you pray for people in the church? When's the last time you prayed for Roger?

SAM: Roger, the pastor? Well, I don't know.

JO: Instead of finding fault with everyone and what they do in the church, why don't you start praying for people?

SAM: I did pray for Dean last week. He asked me to. Had a sinus infection, I think it was.

JO: Well, that's a start, I guess.

DON: Do you know how many sheep it takes to make a Texas sheep cake?

SAM: Can we go somewhere and talk?

JO: Will you listen?

SAM: I have some legitimate complaints about this church, I think.

JO: Okay, let's go talk.

SAM: There are some things I want to get off my chest.

DON: Chess pie. I hope Wilma baked her delicious chess pie.

SANDY: Well, anyway, go to the bake sale. It's for the Lord's work. If you're wondering what this vignette had to do with today's gospel reading, don't worry, Pastor Roger will sort it all out for us and it will be a blessing.

VOICE: Amen!

Many Are Called

Theme

How does God feel about those who reject His Son?

Summary

A mother and father are wondering what to do because they planned a birthday party for their daughter and the children that were invited didn't come. A parable.

Playing Time	3 minutes
Setting	Sheila and Ron's home
Props	None
Costumes	Contemporary, casual
Time	The present
Cast	SHEILA — mother of birthday girl
	RON — her husband
	MADGE — their next door neighbor

MADGE: (*HOLDING THE PHONE BUT TALKING TO SHEILA*) Another busy signal.

SHEILA: So, what am I going to do?

MADGE: Send them all hate mail?

SHEILA: I could do that! I could easily do that. Can you imagine? The nerve, the unmitigated, completely regurgitated nerve. I don't believe I've ever been so insulted.

MADGE: What do we do?

SHEILA: How many did you call?

MADGE: Many. I've been on the phone since I got here. Many were called.

SHEILA: How many?

MADGE: I called everyone on the list.

SHEILA: They've insulted my baby. That's what they've done, insulted my baby. Do you know how mad that makes me?

MADGE: It would make any mother mad.

SHEILA: Well, I'm madder.

MADGE: Did you get all the stuff put away?

SHEILA: Yeah, yeah, finally. The ice cream I put in your freezer.

MADGE: Okay, good. What did you do with the pizza?

SHEILA: That's in my freezer.

MADGE: What about Mr. Buttons?

SHEILA: He wouldn't fit in the freezer.

MADGE: Was he angry when you told him the party was canceled?

SHEILA: Was he angry? After coming all the way across town? I paid him anyway.

MADGE: Should I keep calling?

SHEILA: I guess not. They make me so mad, I could ...

RON: (*ENTERS*) Hi, honey, I'm home. Hi, Madge. Where's Claudine?

SHEILA: I'm so angry.

RON: What is it, Hon? What's wrong? (*SHEILA RUNS INTO RON'S ARMS*)

MADGE: Welcome to the clean-up crew for the best birthday party that never was.

RON: Oh, the birthday party. I forgot that was today.

MADGE: So did half the town.

SHEILA: The kids that Claudine invited from her class at school didn't come.

RON: No one came?

SHEILA: Not one person.

RON: Did they call?

SHEILA: No. But I think I'll call them and tell them off. I'm so angry.

MADGE: They've all got their phones off the hook or they're making the biggest conference call in history.

RON: Telling them off — what good would that do?

SHEILA: I'd feel better. And the parents should know how their children act.

RON: I don't think it will do any good.

SHEILA: I want to do it anyway.

MADGE: Yeah, let her do it.

RON: Sheila, listen, the parents of the kids are probably just as snobbish as their children. Where do you think they learn it?

SHEILA: I know. I don't know what we can do. Claudine is very hurt. You know how thirteen-year-olds are.

RON: I'm beginning to find out.

SHEILA: So, your daughter has been insulted. What are you going to do?

MADGE: Yeah, what are you going to do?

RON: I don't know.

SHEILA: Well, do something!

RON: All right. How about this? We'll go to the children's home and take our party things and have a party there.

SHEILA: The children's home? Are you serious?

MADGE: Twelve pizzas? Five gallons of ice cream?

RON: You want a party. I'll bet the orphans at the children's home would love a party.

SHEILA: It might work at that.

MADGE: It would be fun. Claudine would love it.

SHEILA: All right. Let's try it.

RON: I'll call the newspaper and see if they'll send a reporter and a photographer to take some shots of the kids having fun.

SHEILA: And I'll call Mr. Buttons and have him meet us there.

RON: That's perfect, Honey.

SHEILA: Those snobby parents who are always fighting to get their pictures in the paper. They'll be so envious. They'll be pulling their hair.

RON: They'll be weeping.

MADGE: And gnashing their teeth!

SHEILA: Gnashing their teeth?

MADGE AND SHEILA: Yeah!

God And The State

Theme

How do Christians ethically relate to their government?

Summary

They're at it again. They won't give up. The Pharisees are trying to catch Jesus in another trap. This time they think it's fool-proof, the money trap. Will they corner Him and trip Him up on His own words? Very unlikely.

Playing Time	4 minutes
Setting	Jerusalem
Props	A large coin
Costumes	Contemporary, casual
Time	The time of Jesus
Cast	JESUS
	LAWYER
	BRIGHT
	DULL
	DULLER

LAWYER: (*ENTERS ALONG WITH BRIGHT, DULL, AND DULLER*) Okay, okay. All right. Let's quiet down. Now, why are we meeting? To trap this new teacher, Jesus, right? He's becoming too popular. The Temple trade has dropped off. I say it's because of the junk that He is preaching.

ALL: Right.

LAWYER: Nothing we tried has worked yet. Any new suggestions?

BRIGHT: We have to try something. You know what I heard? He's been healing. And I know it can't be true but it is said He raised a synagogue official's daughter from the dead.

DULL: No. It couldn't be true, could it?

BRIGHT: Taxes!

DULL: Yeah. How about taxes? Taxes have always baffled us. They ought to baffle a simple teacher from the country.

ALL: Taxes, yeah. Good idea.

LAWYER: All right. All right. Taxes it is. Now, what do we say?

BRIGHT: Why not the Rheoboam question?

LAWYER: That's a good one.

DULL: How does it go?

BRIGHT: Oh, you remember. "Lighten the yoke upon us. Our taxes are too high." Any teacher who wants a following will say that's what he supports.

DULL: And what if He says He supports reducing our taxes. How will that trap Him? I even support that! Everyone does.

BRIGHT: Of course you do. Everyone does who has to pay them. That's the beauty of this plan. It can't fail to trap Him.

DULLER: Okay, so He says He is for reducing taxes, big deal. This is some trap!

BRIGHT: Don't you get it? He says He's for reducing taxes and we'll say, "Oh, you are not a supporter of the Roman government, eh?"

LAWYER: And if He says He is in favor of high taxes ... well, we will charge Him with blasphemy. It's perfect.

DULLER: Wait. Blasphemy? How?

BRIGHT: Whose head is on the Roman coin? (*PRODUCING COIN*)

DULLER: I refuse to say it.

BRIGHT: Of course you do. He claims to be god. Caesar's claims of divinity are there for all to see.

DULL: Oh, I get it. If Jesus says He supports taxes to Caesar we will charge Him with supporting this self-proclaimed god, Caesar.

BRIGHT: It is perfect. Let's try it on Him right now. I'm very interested to meet with Jesus again.

ALL: Yes, why not. Let's do it.

DULLER: Wait. How will we ever get to talk to Him without making Him suspicious?

LAWYER: We'll have to flatter Him. Set Him up by admitting His fairness with all people. (*JESUS ENTERS*)

BRIGHT: I don't know.

LAWYER: It'll work. You'll see. We'll force Him into a position where He'll have to answer us. (*THEY APPROACH JESUS*) Let me do the talking. I can handle Him — a country preacher. I can outwit Him. Watch this. (*TO JESUS*) Teacher, we know that you are truthful and treat all persons the same but teach how to know God. By the way, I was just thinking, just off the top of my head, mind you, is it lawful to pay the poll tax to Caesar or not?

JESUS: Why are you testing me? You hypocrite. Bring me a coin.

LAWYER: I'm prepared. *(HANDS JESUS A COIN)*

JESUS: Whose likeness and inscription is this?

LAWYER: Caesar's.

JESUS: Pay to Caesar the things that are Caesar's and to God the things that are God's.

LAWYER: Uh, okay. Well, so long. *(JESUS EXITS)*

DULL: *(SARCASTICALLY)* Wow! You really outwitted Him. Oh, that was just great. You really stumped Him that time. I'm so glad I was here to witness that. You really showed Him.

DULLER: I don't even get it. What did He mean?

LAWYER: Will you leave me alone, you ninny! *(HE EXITS)*

BRIGHT: He said the government of men is authorized by God and therefore should be obeyed as far as it has authority, but God's realm is a spiritual one, and in a clash between the two kingdoms God's realm has precedence.

DULLER: He said that?

BRIGHT: Yes, He did. *(BEGINS TO EXIT)*

DULL: Where are you going?

BRIGHT: I'm going to find Jesus. I want to learn more. *(HE EXITS, FOLLOWED LATER BY OTHERS)*

David The Giant Killer

Theme

King David, the ancestor of the Messiah, Jesus, trusted God.
Can we?

Summary

A fun look at the David and Goliath tale, told in an anachronistic, robust manner.

Playing Time	8 minutes
Setting	The Holy Land
Props	Chorus — helmet, crown, pom poms
	Jesse — child's lunch box
	Eliab — rifle
	Messenger — telegram
	Saul — throne
Costumes	Chorus — choir robes
	David — football jersey, Mideast headdress
	Jesse — bib overalls, Mideast headdress
	Eliab — helmet, army fatigues
	Messenger — some outlandish singing telegram outfit
	Saul — crown, robe
Time	The time of David's youth
Cast	CHORUS — a comic group (as many as you want)
	DAVID — a young lad
	JESSE — his father
	ELIAB — David's brother
	GOLIATH — a giant (never seen)
	MESSENGER — singing telegram type
	SAUL — King of Israel

CHORUS: (*ENTERS AND SINGS A PARODY OF THE SPIRITUAL*)
>Little David, play on your harp. Hallelu, hallelu.
>Little David, play on your harp. Hallelu.

Verse 1
>David was a shepherd boy,
>He played his harp and he sang for joy.
>Young David played on his harp. Hallelu, hallelu.
>Young David played on his harp. Hallelu.

(*Repeat chorus*)

JESSE: (*ENTERS*) David! David!

DAVID: (*OFFSTAGE*) Coming, Father. (*DAVID ENTERS*)

JESSE: Are the sheep safe?

DAVID: Yes, they are, Father.

JESSE: Good. (*HANDING DAVID A CHILD'S LUNCH BOX*) Take this food to your brothers and to the commander of their unit. See that everything is well with them. Give them my love.

DAVID: I will, Father.

JESSE: They're fighting against the Philistines in the valley of Elah. Take I-80 West and get off at the Elah exit.

DAVID: I know, Father. We played Elah last year in football. I know where it is.

JESSE: I didn't remember.

DAVID: I scored the winning touchdown, remember?

JESSE: I didn't remember you played football.

DAVID: Of course, Father. I carried the old pigskin, er, I mean, I carried the football for Bethlehem High for the last two years.

JESSE: Lately I forget things. (*JESSE HUGS DAVID*) Well, God go with you, my son.

DAVID: Thank you, Father. See you later. (*JESSE EXITS. DAVID CROSSES TO ANOTHER AREA. CHORUS PUTS ON HELMETS*)

CHORUS:
Verse 2
    Young David went down to war. Hallelu, hallelu.
    Young David went down to war. Hallelu.
    David went to Elah vale,
    And that's where we pick up his trail.
Chorus
    Little David, play on your harp. Hallelu, hallelu.
    Little David, play on your harp. Hallelu.

DAVID: (*SEARCHING FOR HIS BROTHERS*) I wonder where my brothers are? (*DAVID TRIPS OVER ELIAB COWERING ON THE GROUND*)

ELIAB: (*PULLING DAVID DOWN NEXT TO HIM ON THE GROUND*) GET DOWN! Do you want to get us all killed?

DAVID: (*STANDING*) Oh, hi, Eliab. What are you doing down there?

ELIAB: (*PULLING DAVID DOWN*) GET DOWN! You're a sitting duck. They've been throwing in the big stuff, 88s, 105s, GIANTS!

DAVID: (*STANDING*) Giants? The Philistines have giants?

ELIAB: (*STANDING*) Do they ever. And boy, is he a big one.

DAVID: Only one?

ELIAB: One's all they need.

DAVID: How big is he?

ELIAB: I heard he was six cubits and a span.

DAVID: Wow! Nine feet, nine inches.

ELIAB: That's what it is, huh? I was never very good at math. He wears a bronze helmet and armor that weighs five thousand shekels! Can you believe that? Five thousand shekels — how much is 5000 shekels?

DAVID: Two hundred pounds. What has he done, kill a lot of our men?

ELIAB: No, not one, but he sure has scared a lot of our men.

DAVID: Really?

ELIAB: Yes, really, but you're not staying to see him. Get back home to your sheep.

DAVID: Who does he think he is?

ELIAB: Go on home, David, before I get angry. (*WE HEAR THE GIANT'S FOOTSTEPS*) Uh oh, here comes Goliath the Giant now. (*ELIAB DROPS TO THE GROUND AND COWERS SOME MORE. DAVID STANDS TALL*)

GOLIATH: (*ON THE MICROPHONE. ELIAB AND DAVID SEE GOLIATH, NO ONE ELSE NEEDS TO*) No one comes to fight me even today? Am I not a Philistine and you, servants of King Saul? Choose a man for yourselves and let him come down to me. If he is able to fight with me and kill me, then we will become your servants, but if I kill him, then you shall become our servants. Today I confront the army of Israel. Is there not a man that will fight me? (*LAUGHS*) I thought not. (*WE HEAR GIANT'S FOOTSTEPS AS HE EXITS*)

DAVID: Eliab! Eliab! (*DAVID FINDS ELIAB COWERING BEHIND HIM*) Oh, there you are. (*DRAGGING ELIAB TO HIS FEET*) Eliab, why doesn't someone kill him?

ELIAB: Kill him — Goliath — are you kidding?

MESSENGER: (*ENTERS ON ROLLER SKATES*) David! David! Telegram for David!

DAVID: Over here. I'm David.

MESSENGER: (*OFFERING TELEGRAM TO DAVID*) Are you David?

DAVID: Yes.

MESSENGER: The shepherd boy? (*TAKES TELEGRAM BACK*)

DAVID: Yes. That's me.

MESSENGER: Shall I sing it for you? (*SINGING HORRIBLY*) King Saul. King Saul ...

DAVID: (*TAKING TELEGRAM*) Never mind. I'll just read it. (*MESSENGER IS WAITING FOR A TIP*) Do you want a tip? Don't sing anymore. (*MESSENGER EXITS*) Hm. King Saul wants to see me. All right, I'll go see the King. (*DAVID CROSSES TO ANOTHER AREA*)

CHORUS: (*WEARING CROWNS*)
Verse 3
    Young David went to the King. Hallelu, hallelu.
    Young David went to the King. Hallelu.

David was a brave young lad,
Because of the Holy Spirit he had.
Chorus
    Little David, play on your harp. Hallelu, halelu.
    Little David, play on your harp. Hallelu.

SAUL: *(ENTERS, SITS ON THRONE. HE'S A BIT SCHIZO)* *Yes?*

DAVID: You sent for me?

SAUL: I did? Yes, I suppose I did. Well, sit down. Relax. *(DAVID SITS)* What did you want?

DAVID: King Saul ...

SAUL: *(STARTLED)* King Saul? Where?

DAVID: Relax. That's you — King Saul.

SAUL: Oh, yes, that's right. I was just testing. Just testing. What happened?

DAVID: You sent for me.

SAUL: Oh, yes. That's right. Well, what did you want?

DAVID: I didn't want anything.

SAUL: Well, then, why bother me? Get out! Get out!

DAVID: *(DAVID BEGINS TO EXIT BUT HESITATES AND RE-TURNS)* King Saul, I have an idea.

SAUL: *(FULLY RECOVERED)* David, my boy. How are you? *(HUGS DAVID)* Sit down. Sit down, my boy. It's been such a long time. How are you?

307

DAVID: (*SITTING*) Not bad. How are you?

SAUL: Not good. Boy, have I got a problem.

DAVID: That's what I came to see you about. I'm going to kill the giant, Goliath, for you.

SAUL: Giant, schmiant. That's not my problem. Giants are no problem. It's my daughter. No one wants to marry her.

DAVID: I'll marry her.

SAUL: No, no, David. You're like a son to me. I couldn't stick you with her. She's so ...

DAVID: Listen, I'll make you a deal. I'll kill the giant and you give me your daughter. Deal?

SAUL: Deal. (*THEY PERFORM AN ELABORATE HAND-SHAKE. DAVID EXITS AND THEN REENTERS*)

DAVID: Oh, I forgot my lunch.

SAUL: Who are you? What do you want?

DAVID: I forgot my lunch.

SAUL: Who are you?

DAVID: Your almost son-in-law.

SAUL: Did I call for you?

DAVID: Well, not this time. I forgot ...

SAUL: Get out! (*THROWS LUNCH BOX AT DAVID*)

DAVID: Oh, thanks.

SAUL: Wait, do you know David?

DAVID: Quite well, yes.

SAUL: Well, you tell David to wear my armor. That will protect him.

DAVID: Protect me when I fight the giant?

SAUL: Giant, schmiant. The armor will protect him from my daughter. (*SAUL EXITS. DAVID CROSSES TO ANOTHER AREA*)

CHORUS: (*WEARING WAR HELMETS AND MARCHING*)
Verse 4
> Young David went to the war. Halellu, hallelu.
> Young David went to the war. Hallelu,
> David tried the armor of Saul.
> He found it didn't work at all.

Chorus
> Little David, play on your harp. Hallelu, hallelu,
> Little David, play on your harp. Hallelu.

ELIAB: I heard you were going to fight Goliath. Are you mad?

DAVID: No, but I am a bit angry. Saul gave me his armor to wear and I wasn't used to it, so I'm going to use my stick and my sling. I'll just take along these five smooth stones.

ELIAB: That's it? Five smooth stones?

DAVID: Let me tell you something. Whenever I was tending my sheep and a lion or a bear would attack my flock and carry off one of my sheep, I would catch him and kill him with my bare hands. I have killed both the lion and the bear. This giant is no better than they are since he taunted the armies of the living God. The Lord delivered me from the paws of the lion and the paws of the bear. He will deliver me from the paws, er, I mean the hands of the Philistine.

309

CHORUS: (*PRAYERFULLY*)
Verse 5
  Young David faced the giant. Hallelu, hallelu.
  Young David faced the giant. Hallelu.
  David fought the giant alone.
  He wasn't scared 'cause the Lord he'd known.
Chorus
  Little David, play on your harp. Hallelu, hallelu.
  Little David, play on your harp. Hallelu.

GOLIATH: (*WE HEAR HIS FOOTSTEPS*) You must be David.

DAVID: Yes, how did you know?

GOLIATH: (*INDICATING CHORUS*) Those girls over there have been singing about you. (*THE CHORUS GIGGLES AND WAVES TO DAVID*) David, am I a dog that you come to me with a stick?

DAVID: Are you asking for my opinion?

GOLIATH: I curse you by all the gods of the Philistines.

DAVID: That's a lot of cursing. Should you be cursing? This is a mixed audience, you know. (*THE CHORUS GIGGLES AND WAVES*)

GOLIATH: Oh, excuse me, ladies. But you, David, you come here and I'll give your flesh to the birds of the air and the beasts of the field.

DAVID: You come against me with a sword and a spear but I come against you in the name of the Lord, Almighty, the God of the armies of Israel, whom you have defied. This day the Lord will hand you over to me and I'll strike you down and cut off your head. I will give the carcasses of your army to the birds of the air and the beasts of the earth. And then the whole world will know that there is a God in Israel. All those gathered here will know that it is not by the sword or spear that the Lord saves, for the battle is the Lord's and He will give all of you into our hands. *(SOUND EFFECTS: GOLIATH MOVES CLOSER TO DAVID. DAVID REACHES INTO HIS POUCH AND DRAWS OUT A STONE AND FITS IT INTO HIS SLING AND WHIRLS IT AROUND HIS HEAD AND LETS IT GO AND GOLIATH FALLS WITH A MIGHTY EARTH-SHAKING CRASH)*

CHORUS: *(JOYFULLY, AS CHEERLEADERS WITH POM POMS)*
Verse 6
    Brave David killed Goliath. Hallelu, hallelu.
    Brave David killed Goliath. Hallelu.
    David is a hero, now.
    The Lord our God, He showed him how.
Chorus
    Little David, play on your harp. Hallelu, hallelu.
    Little David, play on your harp. Hallelu.
(THERE IS GREAT MERRIMENT AS DAVID IS LED OFF BY THE CHORUS)

311

In His Debt

Theme
What is the motive behind our gifts to God?

Summary
Two people bring gifts to the altar and are questioned by a third mysterious person as to their intentions.

Playing Time	4 minutes
Setting	Your church
Props	Two gifts
Costumes	Appropriate for church
Time	The present
Cast	MARLA — gift giver
	LES — another gift giver
	GUY — a questioner

MARLA: (*PLACING A GIFT ON THE ALTAR*) I give you this gift, Lord, with all my heart.

GUY: (*RISING FROM BEHIND THE ALTAR AND PEERING OVER*) Wait. Wait just a minute. What are you doing?

MARLA: I'm bringing a gift to God.

GUY: (*CROSSING AROUND ALTAR TO CONFRONT HER*) Why?

MARLA: Why? What do you mean, "why?"

GUY: I just wanted to know why you are doing this — bringing a gift to God.

MARLA: I thought it would be appropriate to bring God a gift.

GUY: Where did you learn that?

MARLA: Well, I don't know. From the Bible, I think.

GUY: Where in the Bible?

MARLA: Well, I don't know. I really don't know.

LES: Is this guy giving you a hard time, Miss?

MARLA: Well, I don't know the Bible that well. But I did want to bring my gift to the altar.

LES: Listen, guy, why not butt out. This lady is bringing her gift and I, for one, don't think you should be bothering her.

GUY: I was just asking what her intentions are.

LES: Yeah, and I'm saying, don't butt in.

GUY: I see you're bringing a gift, too.

LES: Very observant.

GUY: Why do you bring a gift to God?

LES: Are you a trouble maker?

GUY: I seem to be making difficulties, but I don't wish to. I was merely asking what your intentions are in bringing a gift to God.

LES: Okay, wise guy, how about Malachi 3:10 — "Bring the whole tithe into the storehouse."

GUY: Oh, then this is your tithe. I see then, that explains it. Well, thanks. I'm sure the church can use it.

MARLA: This isn't my tithe. I already gave my tithe. This is just a gift.

LES: Now, you just wait a minute. What right have you to question what the lady wants to give to God?

GUY: I was questioning her intentions.

LES: All right, her intentions then. What right do you have to question her intentions? If she wants to bring a gift she can bring it.

GUY: Very true. I was asking why she brought it. And I haven't received an answer. I don't think either one of you know why you brought your gifts.

LES: This is the altar of God, isn't it?

GUY: It is.

LES: Well, I just want to honor God with this gift.

GUY: I don't think so.

LES: You don't think so! You don't think so! So, who cares what you think?

GUY: Maybe no one, but I still don't think you know why you brought these gifts.

LES: Well, I, I don't have to know why. I just brought my gift, and that's all you need to know.

GUY: No, not really. For instance, what if you brought your gift so you could show off in front of someone, say this lady, for example.

LES: You got the wrong guy there.

GUY: Or you simply need a tax write-off.

LES: It's legal.

GUY: Or you gave because you would feel guilty if you didn't.

LES: I remember a scripture. How about Romans 12:1: "Present your bodies a living sacrifice ..."

GUY: You're not presenting your body, are you?

MARLA: I'm not.

LES: Well, neither am I.

GUY: Okay, then, why have you come?

MARLA: To give something to God.

GUY: What does God need?

LES: What?

GUY: I said, what does God need?

LES: Well, nothing, I guess. He is God.

GUY: Right. He is complete within Himself.

MARLA: I get it. Then God doesn't need our gifts.

LES: I guess not. (*HE BEGINS TO EXIT*)

GUY: Wait a minute. Why not leave your gift on the altar and go and think about your intentions.

MARLA: All right. (*SHE LEAVES HER GIFT AND BEGINS TO EXIT*)

LES: No way. How am I going to know how it's being used?

GUY: Then you care about how the gift is administered?

LES: Of course I do. I worked hard for that money and I expect it to do the most good in God's Kingdom.

GUY: Would you say there are some strings attached?

LES: Why, no. I just want to make sure that it's used correctly.

GUY: If it's a gift, your responsibility is to bring it. When you leave the gift it is no longer your responsibility.

MARLA: You know, I think I've changed my reason for bringing a gift.

GUY: You have?

LES: Don't let this guy confuse you.

MARLA: I'm not confused. I really want to give something to God because I love Him so much.

GUY: You are the most frustrating individual I have ever met.

MARLA: He loved me so much to take my sins I certainly want to show Him how much I love Him.

GUY: You're serious.

MARLA: Very serious.

GUY: I think you have received something in return.

MARLA: Yes, I have.

GUY: (*AS SHE EXITS*) I knew your heart. I just wanted you to know.

LES: And how about me?

GUY: What about you?

LES: Tell me about my intentions.

GUY: You already know them.

LES: I do?

GUY: Of course you do. You like to hide your real motives.

LES: I do, eh?

GUY: Yes, you do. You're selfish and that's why you are bringing your gift.

LES: That's ridiculous. Just by bringing my gift I am proving I'm not selfish.

GUY: Certainly not. The reason you brought your gift is in your heart and the reason is you're selfish. You thought by giving your gift God would be in your debt. Well, it doesn't work like that. We are eternally in His debt.

317

LES: Well, if that's your attitude I'm leaving and I'll just take my gift with me. You'll come asking for it someday. You'll see. You'll see. (*HE EXITS*)

GUY: I'll see. Yes, I'll see. (*EXITS*)

No Honeymoon

Theme

We are living as if there are no consequences to our actions. We are unprepared for Christ's return.

Summary

Sandra and Ralph have been living together with the intention of marriage someday. But Ralph finds another woman and has left Sandra. Sandra convinces him to go to see their pastor, Rev. Anton, to see if he can help them get back together.

Playing Time	5 minutes
Setting	Rev. Anton's study
Props	None
Costumes	Contemporary, casual
Time	The present
Cast	SANDRA
	RALPH
	REV. ANTON

REV. ANTON: (*ENTERS AND NERVOUSLY ARRANGES CHAIRS. SANDRA ENTERS*) Come on in, Sandra. Have a seat.

SANDRA: (*DISTRAUGHT, PACING*) I can't sit, Rev. Anton.

REV. ANTON: Coffee?

SANDRA: No. No, thanks.

REV. ANTON: Did Ralph say he was coming?

SANDRA: Yes, yes, he did. I phoned him. He said he would. I hope he does.

REV. ANTON: Good. Good.

SANDRA: What am I supposed to do, Rev. Anton? What am I ...

REV. ANTON: Why not just relax. Just sit down and when Ralph gets here maybe we can work this out between you two. (*SANDRA SITS BUT NOT COMFORTABLY. RALPH ENTERS, SHAKES HANDS WITH REV. ANTON BUT PAYS NO ATTENTION TO SANDRA. RALPH IS CONFIDENT IN HIS POSITION AND HAS NO COMPASSION FOR SANDRA. SANDRA RISES NER-VOUSLY, AWAITING SOME SIGN THAT RALPH IS READY TO RECONCILE. HE ONLY NODS IN HER DIRECTION WHICH MAKES HER CRY*) Well, Ralph, thank you for coming.

RALPH: No problem.

REV. ANTON: Won't you both sit? (*NO ONE SITS*)

RALPH: I can't stay long.

REV. ANTON: As I said, thanks for coming.

RALPH: Sure.

REV. ANTON: I thought we could all talk a little and see if there wasn't some way we could work this out.

RALPH: I doubt it. (*SANDRA CRIES*)

REV. ANTON: I think I'll sit. There, now. Now, let's see — it seems like you two were working toward, ah, toward ah, something permanent in your relationship. (*SANDRA CRIES*)

RALPH: Listen, if she's going to do a lot of this I don't see any point in me ...

REV. ANTON: Sandra, we need to talk, here. Do you think you could try to calm down a little bit so we can get to the bottom of this problem.

SANDRA: You don't know, Rev. Anton. You don't have any idea.

RALPH: (*BEGINNING TO EXIT*) I've got lots to do.

REV. ANTON: (*RISING AND STOPPING RALPH WITH A HAND ON HIS SHOULDER*) Please, Ralph. Just sit. Please. (*RALPH SITS BUT LOOKS AS IF HE WILL BOLT ANY MINUTE*)

SANDRA: Do you know what he did?

RALPH: Oh, boy, here it all comes now.

REV. ANTON: (*GUIDING SANDRA TO A SEAT*) Sandra, why don't you sit here. (*HANDING HER A BOX OF TISSUES AND RETURNING TO HIS SEAT AND SITTING*) Now, maybe we can talk. I remember the last time you came to church you both said you were going to get married. You seemed so excited about the wedding.

SANDRA: That was last month.

REV. ANTON: And now you're not getting married, is that right?

RALPH: No, we're not.

REV. ANTON: What changed your minds?

SANDRA: You said you loved me.

REV. ANTON: Sandra, please. Now, maybe I can find out a little more about you two. What was it that you saw in each other. Sandra? (*SANDRA CRIES*) No, let's let Ralph start.

RALPH: Huh?

REV. ANTON: I said, what was it that attracted you to Sandra?

RALPH: Oh, I can't remember. (*SANDRA CRIES*)

REV. ANTON: Sandra? Sandra? Maybe you can start. What first attracted you to Ralph?

SANDRA: (*THROUGH SOBS*) I remember, I first saw him coming out of the men's locker room. He was on the basketball team. He was really a hunk. He ran onto the floor and looked at me just before he shot the ball.

RALPH: I never looked at you.

SANDRA: You did. You looked right at me. It was love at first sight.

RALPH: I never did.

REV. ANTON: Well, now, Sandra has got the ball rolling, so to speak. How about you, Ralph? What did you like about Sandra?

RALPH: Sandra? Well, I guess she looked okay.

REV. ANTON: Well, you see. There's a start. And what else?

RALPH: What else? I don't know. Hey! I don't have time for this!

REV. ANTON: I think we were getting somewhere. Now, let's not get too excited. Can we get back to the question?

SANDRA: He told me he loved me.

RALPH: I thought I did. I meant it at the time I said it, I guess.

REV. ANTON: And what about now?

RALPH: No, I don't love her now. Not anymore.

SANDRA: (*JUMPING UP*) You said you loved me.

REV. ANTON: (*RISING AND GUIDING SANDRA BACK TO HER SEAT*) And you still love Ralph. (*REV. ANTON SITS*)

SANDRA: Of course I do. I love you, Ralph.

RALPH: Oh, brother.

REV. ANTON: (*TO RALPH*) Well, then, why did this love end?

RALPH: Well, I ...

SANDRA: He left me for another woman.

REV. ANTON: (*TO RALPH*) You've found someone else?

RALPH: Yes, I have found someone else.

SANDRA: But you said you loved me.

RALPH: I'm sorry I said it.

SANDRA: But, why? Why can't you love me?

RALPH: (*LOGICALLY*) Because I found someone else.

SANDRA: (*CRYING*) Why? Why did this have to happen?

RALPH: (*A PLEA FOR PEACE OR ESCAPE*) Please.

REV. ANTON: Could I have some details, please?

SANDRA: We were going to get married.

REV. ANTON: And what stopped you?

RALPH: We decided not to.

SANDRA: We wanted to live together first.

RALPH: No one buys a new pair of shoes until they try them on. You know what I mean?

REV. ANTON: I see.

RALPH: And it's good we did live together, too. You see what happened.

SANDRA: He said he loved me. Doesn't that mean anything anymore?

REV. ANTON: Well, it should. Let's allow Ralph to answer that question.

RALPH: Answer what?

REV. ANTON: Sandra's question — does "I love you" mean anything anymore?

RALPH: Of course it does.

SANDRA: But not to you.

RALPH: I did love you — in a way I did. I just love Cynthia now. That's all. It's like I didn't know what love was until I met Cynthia.

SANDRA: But, you ... we ... made love.

RALPH: (*LOGICALLY*) But we weren't married. That's the point. If we weren't married it doesn't make any difference, does it?

REV. ANTON: There were certain promises made in the intimate act.

RALPH: But we weren't married. What's the big deal?

SANDRA: What am I supposed to do?

RALPH: (*RISING LOOKING AT HIS WATCH*) You're young. Find someone who loves you. Hey, I look at it like this. We weren't married. So we were in a relationship. So what? So, I took a chance too, right? You could have gone off and found someone. I would be left. You take a chance, that's all. Hey, listen, I have to go. (*BEGINS TO EXIT*)

REV. ANTON: (*RISING*) Ralph. I think we should ...

RALPH: I've got to go. Besides, I have nothing more to say. Someone's waiting for me.

SANDRA: Oh, let him go. He wants to leave me. Let him go. Let him go to his new love. (*RALPH EXITS WITHOUT A BACK-WARD GLANCE*)

REV. ANTON: I'm sorry. He has his mind made up, I'm afraid.

SANDRA: (*RISING, PACING*) I had my wedding dress. I told my mother and father.

REV. ANTON: Did Ralph know that?

SANDRA: No. I never told him. I didn't want to pressure him to get married.

325

REV. ANTON: You wanted to be married then?

SANDRA: Yes, of course. Doesn't every girl?

REV. ANTON: And you settled for just living together?

SANDRA: I thought it would just happen some day. I just thought we'd get married. It's all right, Rev. Anton. It's all right. He's right. We weren't married, so how can I expect him to be committed to me?

REV. ANTON: I'm so sorry, Sandra.

SANDRA: So am I. (*SHE EXITS. REV. ANTON SITS*)

The Parable Of Big Business

Theme

In the Kingdom of God increased responsibility necessitates increased faithfulness.

Summary

The boss delegates responsibilities before he leaves and each of his assistants handles the responsibility according to his level of faith and obedience. The first two people receive praise for their efforts when the boss returns, but the last person receives no praise because he wasted his time.

Playing Time	8 minutes
Setting	The boss's office
Props	Files, notebooks, phones, a gun
Costumes	Business
Time	The present
Cast	BOSS
	CELIA — his secretary
	BANNON
	KRASKY
	WHITE

BOSS: (*IS SEATED CENTER STAGE. CELIA STANDS NEARBY*) Are all the accounts paid up?

CELIA: Yes, Sir. Every one of them.

BOSS: Good. That's good. Is my car ready?

CELIA: It has arrived, Sir.

BOSS: Did you contact Bannon, Krusky, and White?

CELIA: I certainly did. They're outside waiting for you.

BOSS: Good. Send them in. I'll be with you in a moment. (*CELIA EXITS. BANNON, KRUSKY AND WHITE ENTER*)

BOSS: All right, boys, you know I'm leaving, so I'm dividing the entire operation between you three. Now, you, Bannon, I'm assigning you to the waterfront operation and the garment district.

BANNON: I'll take good care of things, Boss.

BOSS: I'm not finished, yet. Plus, you also take care of all the theaters and the motels and the car dealership.

BANNON: Gotcha.

BOSS: Okay, get to it. My secretary will have all the details for you in writing.

BANNON: Thanks, Boss. Good luck. (*HE EXITS*)

BOSS: And now, Krusky, you get the nite clubs and the hotel.

KRUSKY: All right, Boss. I'm on my way.

BOSS: Good. Take care.

KRUSKY: Will do, Boss. You, too.

BOSS: And now you, White.

WHITE: Sir?

BOSS: I'm putting you in charge of the deli.

WHITE: The deli, Sir?

BOSS: Yes, you used to work there so you know the operation. (*HANDS HIM THE DEED*) It's yours until I return. Now, I don't want to be late, so take care. I'll see you later. (*BOSS EXITS*)

WHITE: Okay. (*SITS IN BOSS' CHAIR*)

KRUSKY: (*ENTERS. ON PHONE*) Thanks, Mason. Get back to me on that, will you?

CELIA: (*ENTERS*) Mr. Krusky, here are those files you wanted on the copper mining deal.

KRUSKY: Thanks, Celia. Oh, by the way, did the Boss mention anything about buying into soft drinks?

CELIA: Soft drinks? No, he didn't. (*KRUSKY AND CELIA CROSS TO ANOTHER AREA. KRUSKY TALKS ON PHONE*)

BANNON: (*ENTERS. AS HE DOES, CELIA CROSSES TO HIM*) Celia? Remember the Maitlin Company. Well, I think I can buy them out. They had a bad month and they're desperate. I've got some ideas that will help them turn a profit. Get me all the facts on them, will you? (*BANNON AND CELIA CROSS TO ANOTHER AREA. BANNON GETS ON PHONE*)

WHITE: (*THINKING OUT LOUD*) Look at them. Of course they're doing well. Look at all they have to work with. What did I get? The deli, that's what. It never did make any money. Why the boss didn't get rid of it long ago, I'll never know.

CELIA: Mr. Bannon, those statistics just came in on Stryker Oil.

BANNON: Good. Let's have a look. (*INTO PHONE.*) Listen, H. C., I don't think ...

WHITE: I can't even think straight. All this noise. What am I supposed to do? I can't sell the deli, what if the boss comes back and doesn't like what I did?

KRUSKY: Celia, ask the managers of the Alkin Company. to stand by, will you? I'll talk to them later.

CELIA: Mr. Krusky, will you be dining out tonight?

KRUSKY: No. Too much work. Send out for Chinese.

WHITE: You'd think they'd at least eat at the deli. Naw! I wouldn't even eat there. It's hopeless. No one would buy the place. It doesn't make a dime and it's run down. How'd I get stuck with such a lousy place? When the boss comes back, I'm going to ... but what if the boss doesn't come back? I've heard rumors that he's going away because of his heart. Maybe he'll kick-off. Maybe I could close the deli down and if he doesn't come back I could sell the land, maybe keep the money myself. I'll just hide this deed ... (*TIME PASSES. BANNON, KRUSKY AND CELIA MOVE IN FAST MOTION AND WHITE SITS LAZILY IN BOSS' CHAIR*)

BANNON: How long has it been since the boss left?

CELIA: Three and a half years.

BANNON: Well, I just hope, when he gets back ... (*THE BOSS ENTERS*)

CELIA: Mr ...

BANNON: Boss, you're back.

KRUSKY: (*RUSHING UP TO HIM*) Welcome home. It's been a long time.

BANNON: How was it?

BOSS: Well, I made a few good deals. How about here? How'd it go?

BANNON: I had to sell Sinco, but I bought Northco Inc. and the Wintime Camera.

BOSS: And how are they doing?

BANNON: Wintime had a twenty percent increase so far this year. Here's the rest of the statistics. We doubled our holdings.

BOSS: Well done. Good. Very good. How would you like to oversee the entire operation here?

BANNON: I'd like the opportunity.

BOSS: Why don't you get started. There's a bonus in it, too. You've been faithful.

BANNON: Thanks a lot. (*HE EXITS*)

KRUSKY: Look at this. I'm glad you're here. I didn't know whether to buy the coal interest in the Worthy Company or their oil stock.

BOSS: Where'd you get the capital for this?

KRUSKY: We did really well last year. (*HANDS HIM A FOLDER*)

BOSS: I guess so. In that case, buy them both. Try to close the deal within a couple of days; I'm promoting you. I want you to be in charge of the operation in Paris.

KRUSKY: Thanks, Boss. (*HE EXITS*)

WHITE: Boss?

BOSS: Oh, yes, White. What is it? How's the deli?

WHITE: That's what I wanted to talk to you about.

BOSS: Well?

WHITE: The deli wasn't doing so good.

BOSS: Go on.

WHITE: It lost money two years in a row, and I ...

BOSS: Lost money! How did that happen?

WHITE: How'd it happen? I don't know. No customers, I guess.

BOSS: You guess! No one guesses around me. Especially when money's involved.

WHITE: I was afraid. I hid the deed so no one would steal the property from you. I know you're a hard man in business, so ...

BOSS: (*GRABBING WHITE BY THE COLLAR*) Why, you lazy, good for nothing ... You ought to have sold it and at least put the money in the bank where it would've drawn interest.

WHITE: But you've got lots of money. What could one little deli mean to you?

BOSS: You're right. I've got lots of money and I intend to have a lot more, but I haven't held onto it by being lazy ... or hiring lazy people to work for me. (*YELLS*) Bannon, Krusky! (*THEY ENTER. CELIA FOLLOWS*)

BANNON: Yes, Sir?

BOSS: (*HANDING DEED TO BANNON*) Here, take this. It's the deli. You're in charge of it now.

BANNON: Good. I've got some things I'd like to try, there.

BOSS: And take care of this lazy ... (*HANDING WHITE OVER TO BANNON AND KRUSKY WHO EXIT WITH HIM*)

CELIA: Sir?

BOSS: Yes?

CELIA: May I ask a question?

BOSS: Of course. Go right ahead.

CELIA: I can understand your getting rid of Mr. White. I would have done the same thing myself. But why did you give the deli to Mr. Bannon?

BOSS: Well, it's like this — it all boils down to responsibility. If you can't handle the little things ...

CELIA: You can't handle the big things, right?

BOSS: Right. And it has a lot to do with accountability. White must have thought there would never come a time when I would call him to account. Who knows what was going on in his mind? (*BANNON AND KRUSKY ENTER*)

CELIA: Too bad.

BOSS: Yeah. (*A PISTOL SHOT*)

The Glory Of The Lord

Theme
To God be the glory.

Summary
The voices of all creatures praise the Lord. A reader's theatre production.

Playing Time	7 minutes
Setting	Eternity
Props	Folders from which to read
Costumes	Black
Time	Eternity
Cast	EIGHT READERS

(READERS ENTER AND TAKE THEIR PLACES)

FIRST MAN: On the Lord's day I was in the Spirit and I heard behind me a loud voice like a trumpet ... I turned around to see the voice that was speaking to me and when I turned I saw seven golden lampstands, and among the lampstands was someone "like a son of man," dressed in a robe reaching down to his feet and with a golden sash around his chest. His head and hair were white like wool, as white as snow, and his eyes were like blazing fire. His feet were like bronze glowing in a furnace, and his voice was like the sound of rushing waters. In his right hand he held seven stars, and out of his mouth came a sharp double-edged sword. His face was like the sun shining in all its brilliance. When I saw him, I fell at his feet as though dead. Then he placed his right hand on me and said:

SECOND MAN: Do not be afraid. I am the first and the last. I am the Living One; I was dead, and behold I am alive forever and ever! And I hold the keys of death and Hades.

FIRST MAN: After this, I looked, and there before me was a door standing open in heaven. And the voice I had first heard speaking to me like a trumpet said:

SECOND MAN: Come up here, and I will show you what must take place after this.

FIRST MAN: At once I was in the Spirit. I looked and I saw a windstorm coming out of the north — an immense cloud with flashing lightning and surrounded by brilliant light. The center of the fire looked like glowing metal, and in the fire was what looked like four living creatures.

FIRST WOMAN: In appearance their form was that of a man, but each of them had four faces and four wings.

SECOND WOMAN: Their legs were straight; their feet were like those of a calf and gleamed like burnished bronze.

THIRD MAN: Under their wings on their four sides they had the hands of a man.

THIRD WOMAN: All four of them had faces and wings, and their wings touched one another. Each one went straight ahead; they did not turn as they moved.

FOURTH MAN: Their faces looked like this: each of the four had the face of a man, and on the right side each had the face of a lion, and on the left side the face of an ox, each also had the face of an eagle. Such were their faces.

FOURTH WOMAN: Their wings were spread out upward; each had two wings touching the wings of the creatures on either side and two wings covering its body.

SECOND WOMAN: Each one went straight ahead. Wherever the Spirit would go, they would go, without turning as they went.

THIRD WOMAN: The appearance of the living creatures was like burning coals of fire or like torches.

THIRD MAN: Fire moved back and forth among the creatures; it was bright, and the lightning flashed out of it.

FOURTH MAN: The creatures sped back and forth like flashes of lightning.

FIRST MAN: As I looked at the living creatures, I saw a wheel on the ground beside each creature with its four faces.

FOURTH WOMAN: This was the appearance of the structure of the wheels: they sparkled like chrysolite, and all four looked alike. Each appeared to be made like a wheel intersecting a wheel. As they moved they would go in any one of the four directions the creatures faced; the wheels did not turn about as the creatures went.

FIRST WOMAN: Their rims were high and awesome, and all four rims were full of eyes all around

THIRD MAN: When the living creatures moved, the wheels beside them moved; and when the living creatures rose from the ground, the wheels also rose. Wherever the Spirit would go, they would go, and the wheels would rise along with them, because the spirit of the living creatures was in the wheels.

SECOND WOMAN: Spread out above the heads of the living creatures was what looked like an expanse, sparkling like ice and awesome.

THIRD WOMAN: Under the expanse their wings were stretched out toward one another.

FOURTH WOMAN: When the creatures moved, I heard the sound of their wings, like the roar of rushing waters, like the voice of the Almighty, like the tumult of an army. When they stood still they lowered their wings.

THIRD MAN: Above the expanse over their heads was what looked like a throne of sapphire and high on the throne was a figure like that of a man.

THIRD WOMAN: I saw that from what appeared to be his waist up he looked like glowing metal, as if full of fire, and that from there down he looked like fire; and brilliant light surrounded him.

FIRST WOMAN: Like the appearance of a rainbow in the clouds on a rainy day, so was the radiance around him. This was the appearance of the likeness of the glory of the Lord.

FIRST MAN: When I saw him I fell face down.

FIRST WOMAN: And the one who sat there had the appearance of jasper and carnelian. A rainbow resembling an emerald, encircled the throne.

SECOND WOMAN: Surrounding the throne were twenty-four thrones, and seated on them were twenty-four elders. They were dressed in white and had crowns of gold on their heads.

THIRD WOMAN: From the throne came flashes of lightning, rumblings, and peals of thunder. Before the throne seven lamps were blazing. These are the seven spirits of God.

THIRD MAN: Also before the throne there was what looked like a sea of glass, clear as crystal.

FOURTH WOMAN: In the center, around the throne, were the four living creatures, and day and night they never stopped saying:

FOUR LIVING CREATURES: Holy, holy, holy is the Lord God Almighty, who was and is, and is to come.

FIRST WOMAN: Whenever the living creatures give glory, honor and thanks to Him who sits on the throne and who lives forever and ever, the twenty-four elders fall down before Him who sits on the throne, and worship Him who lives forever and ever. They lay their crowns before the throne and say:

TWENTY-FOUR ELDERS: You are worthy, our Lord and God, to receive glory and honor and power, for you created all things, and by your will they were created, and have their being.

FIRST MAN: Then I saw in the right hand of Him who sat on the throne, a scroll with writing on both sides and sealed with seven seals. And I saw a mighty angel proclaiming in a loud voice:

MIGHTY ANGEL: Who is worthy to break the seals and open the scroll?

FIRST MAN: But no one in heaven or on earth or under the earth could open the scroll or even look inside it. I wept and wept because no one was found who was worthy to open the scroll or look inside. Then one of the elders said to me:

ELDER: Do not weep. See the Lion of Judah, the Root of David, has triumphed. He is able to open the scroll and its seven seals.

FIRST MAN: Then I saw a lamb, looking as if it had been slain, standing in the center of the throne, encircled by the four living creatures and the elders. He had seven horns and seven eyes, which are the seven spirits of God, sent out into all the earth. He came and took the scroll from the right hand of him who sat on the throne, and when he had taken it, the four living creatures and the twenty-four elders fell down before the Lamb. Each one had a harp and they were holding golden bowls full of incense, which are the prayers of the saints. And they sang a new song:

338

FOUR CREATURES AND TWENTY-FOUR ELDERS: You are worthy to take the scroll and to open its seals because you were slain, and with your blood you purchased men for God from every tribe and language and people and nation. You have made them a kingdom and priests to serve our God, and they will reign on the earth.

FIRST MAN: Then I looked and heard the voice of many angels, numbering thousands upon thousands, and ten thousand times ten thousand. They circled the throne and the living creatures and the elders. In a loud voice they sang:

MANY ANGELS, FOUR CREATURES AND TWENTY-FOUR ELDERS: Worthy is the Lamb, who was slain, to receive power and wealth and wisdom and strength and honor and glory and praise.

FIRST MAN: Then I heard every creature in heaven and on earth and under the earth and on the sea, and all that is in them singing:

EVERY CREATED THING: To Him who sits on the throne and to the Lamb be praise and honor and glory and power forever and ever.

FIRST MAN: After this I looked and there before me was a great multitude that no one could count from every tribe, people and language, standing before the throne and in front of the Lamb. And they cried out in a loud voice:

GREAT MULTITUDE: Salvation belongs to our God, who sits on the throne, and to the Lamb.

FIRST MAN: All the angels were standing around the throne and around the elders and the four living creatures. They fell down on their faces before the throne and worshiped God, saying:

ANGELS AND ELDERS AND CREATURES: Amen. Praise and glory and wisdom and thanks and honor and power and strength be to our God forever and ever. Amen.